DIDN'T MY SKIN USED TO FIT?

MARTHA BOLTON

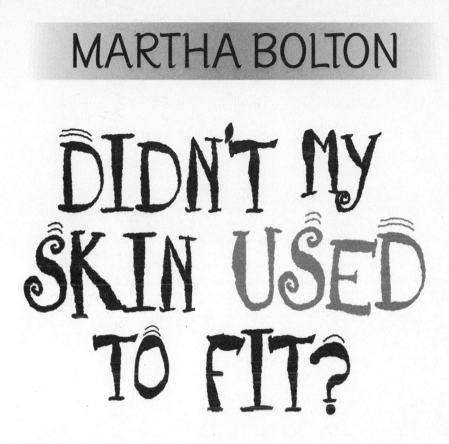

DIDN'T MY SKIN USED TO FIT?

BETHANY HOUSE PUBLISHERS
MINNEAPOLIS, MINNESOTA 55438

Cover illustration by Daniel Vasconsellos
Cover design by Sheryl Thornberg

Published by Bethany House Publishers
A Ministry of Bethany Fellowship International
11400 Hampshire Avenue South
Minneapolis, Minnesota 55438
www.bethanyhouse.com

Printed in the United States of America by
Bethany Press International, Minneapolis, Minnesota 55438

Library of Congress Cataloging-in-Publication Data

Bolton, Martha, 1951–
    Didn't my skin used to fit? : living, laughing, loving life after forty! / by Martha Bolton.
       p.   cm.
    ISBN 0–7642–2184–1
    1. Aging—Humor. 2. Middle age—Humor. I. Title.
PN6231.A43 B65   2000
814'.54—dc21   00–008485
                                                               CIP

To Dr. Robert Rood,
my doctor and friend,
for keeping me together
all these years.

MARTHA BOLTON is a full-time comedy writer and the author of over thirty books. She has been a staff writer for Bob Hope for fifteen years along with writing for Mark Lowry, Bill Gaither, Ann Jillian, Phyllis Diller, and many others. Her material has appeared in *Reader's Digest, Chicken Soup for the Kid's Soul,* and *Brio* magazine, and she has received two Angel awards and both an Emmy nomination and a Dove Award nomination. Martha and her husband live in Tennessee.

ACKNOWLEDGMENTS

A special thanks . . .

To my husband, Russ, whom I met when I was fifteen years old and married when I was eighteen . . . back when my skin used to fit.

To my family: Russ II, Matt, Tony, Nicole, Crystal, and Kiana, who try their best to keep me dressing young and in style. (Now, where did I put those bell-bottoms?)

To my friends Linda Aleahmad and Mary Scott, for never letting a birthday pass without getting our annual dose of laughs. Despite what the rest of our bodies are doing, I'm glad none of us has developed a wrinkle in our sense of humor.

To the memory of my father and mother, Lonnie and Eunice, who taught me how to find the humor in all circumstances . . . even crow's-feet.

To my "adopted" mother, Diantha Ain, whose energy and youthful appearance continue to defy the aging process. What's your secret, Di?

To my editor, Steve Laube, who didn't send even one threatening e-mail while waiting for me to finish this project. (Changing my address four times might have had something to do with that.)

And finally, to all my friends and relatives, who've made this life the wonderful journey it is, I thank you from the bottom of my murmuring heart.

CONTENTS

1

Hangin' Loose

I began noticing it several years ago. The skin I had worn for most—no, make that all—of my life suddenly didn't fit anymore. It used to fit. Rather snugly, as a matter of fact. It was tight around the eyes and mouth. There wasn't any extra under my chin or any hanging down from the sides of my cheeks. There was just enough to make one pass around my entire body. One trip was all that was required, and the exact amount was provided to do the job. Not too much, not too little. It was a perfect fit.

It even stretched. If I gained a pound or two, or twenty, my skin easily expanded to accommodate the increased territory. It wasn't judgmental. It didn't condemn me for that third trip to the food bar. It never tried to knock the brownie out of my hands or shame me into putting back that super-sized scoop of banana pudding. It simply stretched and accommodated. It met the challenge of whatever was required and never once complained.

If I lost weight, my skin was equally accommodating. It would easily return to its original size as though nothing had ever happened. I could gain weight or lose to my heart's content, or discontent, and it would adjust, snapping right back into place when the time was right.

Well, it doesn't snap back anymore. In fact, it doesn't do much of anything except hang there, looser in some places than in others. Like under my chin. That's where a lot of it seems to gather and hang. I'm not very happy about that. It's disconcerting when people stare at my neck and I know they're thinking about Thanksgiving.

Frankly, I think someone should come up with a choker necklace that could be worn just below the chin and would keep all that extra skin tucked neatly in place so it doesn't hang down like loosened upholstery under an antique chair. Whoever designs the first necklace like that will make a fortune.

Little folds of flesh have started to gather around my eyes, too—wrinkles that won't minimize no matter how much wrinkle minimizer I apply. They call it "crow's-feet," but my face doesn't have just a few of them. It has a whole chorus-line thing going on! Every time I squint, my skin seems to fanfold itself into a neat little stack, like pulled taffy, right beside my eyes. It's

14

orderly, but not very attractive. I don't know about you, but I don't want tidy little stacks of pulled taffy next to my eyes. I'd much rather go back to the days when crow's-feet were something you only worried about in an Alfred Hitchcock film.

For some reason, my upper arms have fallen to this extra-skin curse, as well. Don't ask me why, because I haven't a clue. What I do have, though, is a nice swag look every time I raise a hand. I've measured, and there is a good two inches of loose skin under each arm. If a strong wind kicks up, I could be flapping for hours.

I don't think I'd ever actually become airborne, but given the right aerodynamic circumstances, I wouldn't bet against it. That's the reason I wear long sleeves most of the time. They help keep me grounded and save the embarrassment of having to explain a sudden and unscheduled flight to air traffic controllers. What would I say?

"I know I should have radioed in my flight pattern, sir, but this was one of those spur-of-the-moment trips. And besides, that 747 could easily have gone around me."

I'm sure I'd get into some sort of trouble with the Federal Aviation Administration.

Personally, I believe that's why Renaissance clothing sported those long, flow-y sleeves. The women back then had a problem with loose underarms, too.

I've also been noticing the skin beginning to bunch up around my ankles. I thought about painting the little rolls of flesh to match my outfits, passing them off as slouch socks, but decided against it. Even slouch socks aren't supposed to go *that* far up your legs. Besides, if I wear real tight nylons, I can usually push the extra skin back up to my knees, where people *expect* to see extra skin.

Wouldn't it be great if we could unzip our skin, take it to the dry cleaners, and let them shrink it back into shape? They shrink everything else! I suppose that's not an option, though. When's the last time you saw a dry cleaner coupon that read, "While-U-Wait Epidermis Pressing. Save 20%"?

An elderly movie star I once worked with had a good idea. She pulled all the loose face skin up under her bangs, then taped it back by her ears. Amazingly enough, it gave her the illusion of being thirty years younger! I was so impressed with the results, I tried it myself, but it didn't work as well for me. All we had in the house at the time was duct tape, and the silver kept showing through my hair.

Skin that doesn't fit is just one of the symptoms of growing older. There are plenty more, of course. Symptoms that, for the most part, we can't stop no matter how much we'd like to or how hard we try, so we might as well laugh about them. And laughing about them is what this book is all about.

YOU KNOW YOU'RE GETTING OLD WHEN ...

getting "in the groove" means your walker hit a crack in the sidewalk.

2

Yo Quiero
No Discount

I always feared it would happen someday, and there it was—in black and white. All I had done was walk into a Taco Bell in east Tennessee and give my order to the teenager behind the counter.

I wasn't trying to cause any trouble, or pick a fight, or be disruptive in any way. I was just trying to get a couple of tacos and a seven-layer burrito. *That's all.* It was lunch. There was no justification for what the clerk did. He should have handed me my order and let me pay for it, and I would have been on my way. A simple transaction. But *noooo.* This guy had to take it one step further. He had to be confrontational. He had to take it upon himself to ruin my otherwise happy and peaceful day. He had to keep going until he pushed my buttons. All right, *his* button—the one on the cash register *that printed out the words "SENIOR DISCOUNT" on my receipt!*

SENIOR DISCOUNT! I almost dropped my tray! The nerve of that acne-faced troublemaker! Had I not been so hungry, I would have taken him on right then and there. I would have put my tray down, told him to meet me outside, then paper-cut him to a pulp with my birth certificate! I may have been over forty, but I was a *long* way from a senior citizen discount!

But I calmed down, decided to turn the other wrinkle—I mean, cheek—and forgive him. It was a simple oversight, after all. I went ahead and gave him the benefit of the doubt. It was the right thing to do. And besides, *a 10 percent discount is a 10 percent discount!*

Maybe he had a migraine headache and his vision was temporarily impaired, I reasoned. Or maybe it was Taco Bell's own version of *Candid Camera.* That's what that little video camera above the cash register was all about. Or, what was most likely the case, the young man's finger slipped, causing him to inadvertently hit the senior discount key instead of the coupon key. That had to have been it. Both keys were probably in the same general area. One little slip is all it would have taken.

That would have been the end of it, except I realized I

hadn't ordered a drink and had to go back.

"Diet Pepsi, please," I said, watching his every move this time. His finger hit the Diet Pepsi key, then without even getting anywhere near the coupon key, it went straight for the one marked "senior discount." He didn't hesitate for a second. He was confident. He was beyond confident. He didn't even bother to ask my age. If you're in doubt about something, you usually ask first, don't you? Like if you're not sure if someone's pregnant or if she's just put on a few pounds, most people ask before throwing a baby shower. It's the same principle.

But apparently this guy had no doubt. He was so confident I deserved a senior discount, he announced it as he handed the receipt to me.

"Here's your drink, ma'am," he said. "And with the senior discount it comes to $1.09."

I didn't have a choice now. I had to stop him before he dug his hole even deeper.

"*Excuse* me," I said, "but I'm not really a senior. I'm not entitled to a discount. In fact, I shouldn't have gotten a discount on my first order, either."

There, I thought to myself, *I've set the record straight. That should make him think twice before giving away Taco Bell's profits to some other undeserving patron.* I smiled, feeling vindicated and proud of myself that I had made the world a safer place for those of us past the forty mark.

"Aw, close enough," he said. "What's a couple of months?"

It had to be the lighting.

You grow up on the day you have your first
real laugh at yourself.
—Ethel Barrymore

3

Walk a Mile in My Feet

They were by far the most comfortable pair of shoes I'd ever tried on. They were made of soft leather, and their built-up arches supported mine—which, like the Roman Empire, had long since fallen. There was plenty of room to stretch my toes, and they even had tiny air holes that helped the shoes—and my feet—to breathe.

They came in a variety of colors—okay, white, black, and brown—and were available in all the hard-to-find sizes. They weren't cheap, either. About eighty bucks, to be exact. If you want quality, though, you have to pay for it, or at least that's what the salesman kept telling me.

What I'm referring to, of course, is corrective footwear. There, I've said it. I recently had to start wearing corrective shoes because I was developing what is known as a Taylor's bunion on my left foot. I don't even know who Taylor is or why he had the nerve to park his bunion on my foot, but it appears I am stuck with it.

Now, corrective footwear may not represent the latest look on the Paris fashion runways, but who knows, it might catch on someday. And I for one am doing my part to bring corrective footwear into the forefront of the designer world.

I've decided against surgery. Actually my doctors decided against it. Their recommendation was corrective shoes together with a set of custom-made inserts that compensate for every flaw in my feet.

I'm pleased with the results, but let's face it—corrective shoes could use a little updating. They may be comfortable to walk in and give my feet plenty of room, but most of the styles are rather matronly.

We have the power to change that, though. All we bunioned people need to do is *unite*. It's up to us to demand better representation in the fashion world. We need to stand up on our Taylor's bunion, or whoever else's bunion we happen to have, and protest. We deserve stylish sandals and adorable pumps. We're bunioned, not dead. We have the power to make

Dr. Scholl as popular a designer as Bill Blass or Oscar de la Renta. All we need is the chance.

Not only do our feet go through changes as we grow older but our toenails do, as well. In case you haven't noticed it yet, something happens to toenails on a forty-plus body. They start doing what old envelopes do—curl up around the edges and turn yellow. They also tend to thicken and grow to incredible lengths. Howard Hughes' toenails were a perfect example of this. For some unknown reason, he decided to let his toenails and fingernails grow into all sorts of interesting shapes. Maybe he didn't have enough whisks around the house and decided it was just as easy to grow his own.

Long toenails aren't very attractive and limit your choice of footwear, but there are some advantages. Walking barefoot in your backyard could easily take care of that Rototilling job you've been putting off for months. And think of all the fun you can have going swimming and spearfishing at the same time. And then, of course, there are all those cans that you'll be able to open should your electric can opener ever go on the blink.

Other changes that happen to the middle-aged foot have to do with bone structure. Sometimes foot bones start doing strange things when they pass their fortieth birthday. My own feet started growing bony extensions out their sides a few years ago. I'm not sure why they're doing this, but if I ever go to the backwoods of Canada and leave my footprints, we could start a whole new Sasquatch rumor.

Many of the foot problems that we suffer later in life, though, are our own fault. Perhaps they're the result of repeated sports injuries, improper nail care, or years of cramming a size nine foot into a size seven shoe. I used to do that myself, so I guess I shouldn't be surprised if today I've got a Taylor's bunion. In fact, I shouldn't be surprised if I'm carrying around his whole family on my feet. After all, if the shoe fit, I really should have worn it.

If I'd known I was going to live this long, I'd
have taken better care of myself.
—Eubie Blake, at the age of 100

4

And He Huffed and He Puffed . . .

In the story of *The Three Little Pigs*, the big bad wolf gave the three little porkers a threat. He said that if they didn't cooperate and open up their doors, he would huff and puff and blow their houses in.

It's obvious from the verbs "huff" and "puff" that we're talking about a middle-aged wolf here. Middle-aged wolves and middle-aged people do a lot of huffing and puffing. For some of us, it has become a second language. I myself am trilingual—being equally fluent in wheezing.

In our youth, we "huffers" could run, jump, climb, race up stairs, even skip a step or two in the process. We didn't have to make six rest stops in the 100-yard dash or send out for oxygen at the halfway point of a flight of stairs. We could have walked up the steps of the Taj Mahal with very little effort.

As soon as we hit forty, though, it's a different story. A fifteen-step staircase suddenly looks like Mount Everest. Before even attempting to scale something of that magnitude, we search the entire area for an elevator, a ramp, a rope, a search and rescue team, a St. Bernard, anything to make our task easier.

Running, jumping, and stair climbing aren't the only activities that can start us huffing and puffing. We huff and puff getting out of our cars, too, especially if those cars are so low to the ground only an ejection seat could get us out without effort. Frankly, I don't understand why car manufacturers make car seats that low anyway. Maybe it's so that after a test drive the client can't get out and has to buy the car.

Answering the telephone can leave us huffing and puffing, especially if the call comes in the middle of a shower. I'm sure more than a few callers have hung up on a middle-aged huffer, mistaking his gasps for heavy breathing.

A few of us even huff and puff putting on our shoes. You thought tying your shoelaces was a challenge when you were four? Try it when you're forty. That's probably why so many seniors opt for slip-ons. Tying shoelaces just isn't worth the battle.

Opening things can leave us huffing and puffing, too—things like potato chip bags, vacuum-packed cookies, vacuum-sealed cans of cheese puffs, or a membership account at the gym. I don't see why manufacturers have to package their foods so tightly anyway. Is keeping us out of the package the only way they can get away with the nutritional benefits printed on the back?

Now, contrary to what you might think, not all huffers and puffers are smokers . . . or even ex-smokers, for that matter. I'm a huffer even though I've taken very good care of my lungs. I've never smoked and I'm very careful not to inhale too much of my own cooking. And although I did grow up in the Los Angeles smog, I held my breath during most of my formative years. Yet even after taking all these precautions, I still huff and puff. The bottom line is lungs are delicate and susceptible to routine damage over the years no matter what you do to protect them.

So, you see, it had to have been a middle-aged wolf chasing those three little pigs. No teenage wolf would huff and puff that much after going to only three houses. And to huff and puff hard enough to blow two houses in? Why, the poor beast should have been carrying a portable oxygen tank! The story's been told wrong all these years. That wolf didn't want those pigs' houses; he needed mouth-to-mouth resuscitation, and not one of those pigs would help him. Not a good-hearted Babe in the bunch. That poor wolf had to keep going from house to house, huffing and puffing and wheezing. Then, when he finally climbed down the chimney of the third house to personally plead for help, what did they do? They lit a fire in the fireplace, which took up even more oxygen! The story ends there, of course, but it makes its point: middle age? It's rough on both man *and* beast!

YOU KNOW YOU'RE GETTING OLD WHEN ...

the brand new house you remember moving into as a child is now protected by the historical society.

5

Hey, Brother, Can You Spare a 401K?

Many middle-aged people have planned well for retirement. Their savings accounts have grown, their stock investments have paid off, and their retirement plans are all set to kick in. They're prepared.

This chapter is for the rest of us. We who have $2.48 in our savings account, didn't invest in Microsoft because we thought it was a hand cream, and will probably get to our senior years, reach for our nest egg, and realize we already fried it years ago.

I've never been much of a financial wizard. The only portfolio I have is the one I bought at OfficeMax. I have, however, watched everyone around me get rich off their stock market or other investments, while I'm busy looking for a grocery store that has a coin machine where I can cash in my quarters.

Not that my husband and I haven't tried our hand at investing. We have. We just haven't been very successful at it. Take, for instance, the piece of desert property we bought over twenty-five years ago as a retirement investment. It's five and a half acres, and we were told it would eventually be worth well over $100,000.

Today it's not worth much of anything because it has been turned into a sanctuary for an endangered insect. I believe it's in the gnat family. So much for making our fortune there. We've listed it for sale a couple of times, but not many people want to own a government-protected five-and-a-half-acre gnat grazing ground.

Whatever porcelain collectibles I've managed to accumulate over the years haven't paid off either. They actually were increasing in value, but the last Northridge, California, earthquake turned them into mosaic pieces.

How about a game show called *Wheel of Missed Fortunes*? Contestants could spin the wheel for a dollar amount— $10,000, $50,000, $100,000, and so on. A lovely blonde could stand by the answer board while contestants guessed the cost of their missed investment opportunities or bad business decisions. It might be a depressing show for the contestants, but the viewing audience would feel a lot better about their own bad investments.

It's hard to predict which "sure deal" really will be a sure deal. We don't know if a piece of real estate will cost us a fortune or make us one. The stock market carries no guarantees, either. Gold might be devalued; the company handling our retirement account could default; we could be hit with a catastrophic illness that depletes every dime of our savings. There are no fail-safe ways to wealth, no assurances that the money we save is going to be there for us when we need it. That's why the most important investments we can make aren't financial. They are the ones we make in the lives around us.

AN ADVANTAGE OF POVERTY:
Your relatives gain nothing by your death.
—Hebrew proverb

6

Out of Style

I'm not against people dressing younger than their age, but there are some who go to extremes to look young. At some point we have to accept the fact that we're not teenagers anymore. We really *do* need diffused lighting.

Just so there's no misunderstanding, I should clarify that I'm not talking about the person who *acts* young. Being young at heart is a healthy attitude that will add quality to your life and maybe even years.

This chapter is about that individual who blots out her age on her driver's license with Wite-Out, reinvents her personal history to cover her age tracks, and shops in the youth department of clothing stores while complaining to the clerk that the loud music is giving her hearing aid feedback.

I'm glad I don't do things like that. Okay . . . there was that one weekend when my niece, Lisa, gave me a temporary tattoo just above my right ankle. It was one of those fun things you do when your sixteen-year-old niece is staying with you for the weekend. It was a rose in full bloom, but it took several weeks to completely wear off. When people saw it in its varying stages of decomposition, they probably thought I had gotten a real tattoo on the installment plan.

But it was just for fun. Don't get me wrong, I'm not condoning or condemning tattoos. Personally, I'd never get a real one, but that's me. I get enough ink on me when I write. And to be perfectly honest, I can't see varicose veins going that well with body art.

What I am saying, though, is this: In our quest for a more youthful appearance, moderation should be our goal. The following guidelines are provided as a public service:

MIDDLE-AGE FASHION FAUX PAS
The following combinations DO NOT go together:

- A nose ring and bifocals
- Spiked hair and bald spots
- A pierced tongue and dentures
- Bikinis and liver spots
- Miniskirts and support hose

- In-line skates and a walker

- Ankle bracelets and corn pads

- Speedos and cellulite

- A belly button ring and a gall bladder surgery scar

- Unbuttoned disco shirts and a heart monitor

- Hot pants and varicose veins

- Midriff shirts and a midriff bulge

I'm not saying the above is the last word on the subject. Simply use it as a guideline. The fashion police will thank you for it.

All men should strive to learn before they die what they are running from, and to, and why.
—James Thurber

7

Changing With the Times

I've yet to go through the change of life. I know it's coming—those night sweats that flood the lower floor of your home, the hot flashes that keep three fire stations on standby, and the mood swings. Oh, the mood swings—those hormonal changes that make you weep like a baby because Grape-Nuts just went on sale or turn you into a raging lunatic when the telephone cord gets tangled around your ankles.

I'm not looking forward to menopause. Night sweats don't sound like a lot of fun to me. I had them once after a bout with the flu, and it was a lot like taking a shower with your clothes on only the water was coming from the inside out. I prefer the traditional shower. I don't like waking up in a water bed when I didn't start out in one.

And hot flashes—whose idea were those? Frankly, I think they should be called "in-law flashes" since they come totally unannounced and seem like they're never going to leave.

They say irritability is also a common side effect of the change. IRRITABILITY? CAN YOU BELIEVE THAT?! THAT'S THE MOST RIDICULOUS THING I'VE EVER HEARD! THEY'VE GOT NO . . . Sorry. I don't know what came over me.

Men go through a change, too, but they call it a mid-life crisis. Some make it through this period unscathed. Others? Well, you've seen them. Those perfectly stable, well-adjusted men who suddenly go out and buy a Harley-Davidson motorcycle, get a tattoo that says, "AARP RULES," and start listening to the same music they've been telling their kids to turn down for years.

I only mention the Harley-Davidson because it's so symbolic. Many men have their identity tied up in the kind of vehicle they drive. In fact, you can usually tell what stage of life a man is going through by his mode of transportation:

MALE TRANSPORTATION THROUGH THE YEARS

Teenager: take the bus, or ride with your parents
Twenties: borrow Dad's car

Thirties: family van
Forties: sport utility vehicle or truck
Fifties: cherry red convertible capable of going from 0–60
    in two tickets or less
Sixties: Harley with a sidecar for grandchildren
Seventies: fifty-miles-to-the-gallon subcompact vehicle
Eighties: take the bus, or ride with your kids

Now, there's nothing wrong with buying a hot new cherry red convertible or the sleekest motorcycle you can find for your mid-life crisis. But be forewarned: While convertibles and motorcycles can give you that renewed youthfulness and excitement your life has been needing for a long time, you might have to stop every couple of miles or so to go back and pick up your hair.

The meaning of life is to give life meaning.
—Ken Hudgins

8

A Handout

Remember when you were little and someone would ask you your age? You'd hold up three fingers, or four, or five, and say, "This many."

When you get up in years, you still give away your age by your hands, only now it's not intentional. No matter how many face-lifts you undergo, how many laser surgeries you sit perfectly still for, or how much duct tape you've got holding back loose skin, your hands will still betray you. Hands give away age secrets as freely as the rings of a tree trunk or a former best friend.

You could wear gloves, of course, but you might look a little overdressed at your grandson's soccer game. You could keep your hands in your pockets, which is what Napoleon used to do, probably for the same reason, but sooner or later you're going to have to take your hands out to applaud, scratch your nose, or write a check. You can sit on your hands, too. It's not very comfortable and tends to stop the flow of blood, but this is America. You're free to do those kinds of things.

I've also heard lemon juice will help fade age spots, but I don't know how true that is. I tried it once and all it did was make my hands sticky. I don't like sticky hands. I don't mind being friendly, but when I shake someone's hand, I'd like to eventually let go.

A popular dish soap company used to have a mother-daughter team wash dishes together to see if viewers could tell by the look of their dishpan hands which of them was the mother and which was the daughter. It was always difficult to tell since both sets of hands looked terrific. Their soap, they said, was the reason for this. In other words, they were saying to women everywhere that we have to do dishes to get younger looking hands.

I think a husband wrote that commercial.

Age spots, wrinkles, and prominent veins are all telltale signs that we've been putting, as Sheriff John used to say, "another candle on your birthday cake" for quite a while now. And I suppose someday some plastic surgeon will make a lot of money doing wrist lifts or palm pulls to help people hide their age. But until then, I guess our only option is to keep doing those dishes and try to keep our hands as soft and youthful looking as possible. Personally, though, I've given up trying to

hide my age spots. I'm just going to wait for all of them to con-
nect—then I can pass it off as a tan.

What if "Hokey Pokey" really *is* what it's
all about?
—saying on a T-shirt

9

Tan Your Hide

Speaking of tans, I watched a television commercial today for a new instant tanning cream. The pitch seemed to be aimed at those of us who want younger looking skin and are willing to pay three payments of $39.95 each for it. The spokesperson said that a nice golden tan is the secret to looking younger. Face-lifts, laser surgery, and even duct tape were not the answer.

It seems the sun, nature's usual tanning device, does a good job of browning our skin, but it also tends to age it. Harmful sunrays can damage skin so much that instead of our looking younger we actually end up looking older.

The commercial said tanning beds can be harmful to our skin, as well. They didn't have to spend too much airtime talking me out of that. I don't think I'd ever resort to a tanning bed. I'd feel too much like a croissant going into an oven, and since I know all too well what happens to croissants in my oven, I know I'm better off passing on that.

So what's the answer? Well, according to this advertisement, the answer is simple—their instant tanning cream, at $39.95 a month for three months. That's a lot of money, but I'm tempted to order it anyway.

My natural skin tone has always been Clown White, and it'd be fun to have some color for a change. (I'm on the list for a tan transplant, but so far there haven't been any donors.)

So I suppose an instant tanning cream is the only way to go. I just hope they've improved since the days when I was a teenager. I tried one back then and it turned my skin a beautiful shade of Tang orange. I don't think I want to be orange again. It really isn't my color.

But the ad said their instant tanning cream wouldn't do that. In fact, not only did it make those swimsuit-clad fifty-year-old men and women look younger, it also gave them the energy to play a round of beach volleyball. That's some tanning cream!

And while we're on the subject of swimsuits, why doesn't someone make a style that those of us over forty would actually wear? I for one don't like pleats. My skin already has enough pleats; why would I want them in my beachwear? I don't like plunging necklines, either. Enough of me is plunging on its own. And who told anyone that black is the favorite color of those over forty? Our skin might not fit anymore but we're not in mourning over it.

But first things first. No matter what kind of swimsuit I wear, I still need a tan, so I've decided to go ahead and order the tanning cream. And if it doesn't work this time, and I still turn orange, well, I guess that's okay. I live in Tennessee, and orange is one of the colors of the Tennessee State University football team!

Go, Vols!

Therefore we do not lose heart. Though outwardly we are wasting away, yet inwardly we are being renewed day by day.
—2 Corinthians 4:16, NIV

10

Infomercial Paradise

Some say the older you get the less sleep you need. At fifty, you might be getting by on only six or seven hours of sleep. By the time you reach sixty, four or five hours may be all you need. Get to seventy, and not only are you staying awake at night watching every infomercial on television, you're probably squeezing in a 3:00 A.M. trip to the twenty-four-hour Wal-Mart, too.

One reason we require less sleep as we grow older could be all the naps we take throughout the day. I'm not talking about those after-lunch comas that hit people of all ages. I'm talking about that uncontrollable dozing off that seems to hit middle-aged people without warning. It's that overwhelming urge to get in a few winks, whether you're having a root canal, talking on the telephone, or running for a bus.

My husband takes a lot of naps. He can sleep virtually any-where, but his lounging areas of choice are the sofa, the easy chair, the car, the floor, the pew, airline seats, the desk at business meetings, and once in a while, the bed. He can get by on a twenty-minute nap here, a thirty-minute nap there, and only four or five hours of sleep at night.

Another reason we sleep less as we grow older is because we know the party's almost over and we don't want to miss out on a single thing. It's the same reason football fans stay at the game until the very end, even when their team's losing 49–0. It's why people don't sleep through the last fifteen minutes of a good movie. They're afraid they'll miss the best part.

Do the math. If we're in our forties now and are lucky enough to have the genes to make it to our eighties, our lives are already half spent. We should be savoring these days, hours, minutes, even seconds, not sleeping through them. Who wants to oversleep and wake up just in time to hear, "Your life will be closing in ten minutes. Please take all your purchases to the nearest counter and exit through the main doors on your left"?

Life's too important to snooze our way through it. There's too much to do, too much to see, too much to be a part of. If the food processor they're featuring on that 3:00 A.M. infomercial really does dice, slice, chop, mince, puree, and provide therapeutic counseling for my vegetables, I want to know about it. If there's a store open twenty-four hours within a ten-mile radius of my house, I'm going to be out there in the wee hours of the morning supporting it. After all, the people working in the twenty-four-hour Wal-Marts and Kmarts, all-night restaurants, and gas stations are no doubt just like us. They're trying to stretch every moment they've got left, too. I think "Attention Kmart shoppers" has a subliminal message. It's a code for "Life's too short. Stop and smell the roses . . . in our Garden Center at the rear of the store, for $12.98 a dozen."

Time is going to steadily tick by—ticktock, ticktock—and there's nothing we can do to stop it or slow it down. If we're going to live this life to its fullest, and if we're going to do the work that God has for us to do, we need to do it now, not later—today, not tomorrow. After all, we don't want to get to the pearly gates and have to stand before God and say, "Sorry, Lord, I was sleeping. Can you tell me what it was I missed?"

The tragedy of life is not that it ends so soon,
but that we wait so long to begin it.
—Anonymous

11

Making Memories, Not Regrets

My mother dreamed her whole life of going to Washington, D.C. Almost every summer my family traveled from our home in California to Arkansas, where my grandparents lived. One of those summers we probably could have driven up to Washington, D.C., and fulfilled her lifelong dream, but we never did. For whatever reason (no doubt financial), she denied herself that pleasure.

When my father passed away, the one regret I had was that I had not taken him on more trips. So after his death, I made a vow to myself that my mother would see Washington, D.C. Fulfilling that dream didn't come easy. I had to save the money, make adjustments to my work schedule, book all the necessary flights and hotels, and—hardest of all—get Mother to agree to the vacation. She thought she couldn't take that much time off work. I tried to convince her that she could, but when that didn't work, I called her boss and arranged for her to have the time off, then basically "kidnapped" her.

We had a wonderful time visiting the White House, the Capitol, the FBI headquarters, Arlington Cemetery, the Smithsonian, and just about everything else there is to see there. And although the trip took some extra effort and planning, it was well worth it. The pictures and memories I have of our time together are irreplaceable.

After that trip, I planned as many weekend jaunts with my mom to as many different places as I could. These trips quickly became a highlight of both our lives.

A few years ago I decided to fulfill one of my own lifelong dreams. I had always wanted to see the Indian dwellings at Mesa Verde, Colorado. Using the same strategy I had used with my mother, I decided I was going to *make* it happen. I would create my own memories instead of waiting for them to come to me. I saved the money, made the arrangements, and soon my family and I were standing among Indian ruins. Seeing those dwellings gave me a sense of completeness. Once again I had made a memory instead of a regret.

Life is unpredictable. My mother's life came to an end before any of us expected. She was seventy-two and, except for the lymphoma, which had only appeared eight months before, she had hardly been sick a day in her life. I miss her terribly, but every time I run across my pictures of our trips together, they remind me of a few of her dreams that I didn't allow to die with her.

Where is it that you've always wanted to go? What is it you've always wanted to do? Is there some place you've longed to take a loved one? Quit making excuses. Make plans, make the sacrifices, and do it!

Life is made up of ever so many partings
welded together.
—Charles Dickens

12

Gravy Is Not a Food Group

It doesn't matter how many deep-fried onion rings we've consumed over the years, how many pecan pies we've inhaled, or how much gravy we've allowed to dam up our arteries, when we pass forty, all of a sudden we become obsessed with eating healthy foods. We don't necessarily change our diet, but we become obsessed with the *idea* of changing it.

It's all those public service announcements that start getting to us:

> Ben thought he was going to live forever. He believed he was invincible. He was convinced his fatty, cholesterol-filled, salt-laden diet wasn't hurting him. Ben was wrong. At

forty-three, he now has to work at home. His desk at his job wasn't equipped to handle the life-support apparatus. Don't be like Ben. Don't wait until it's too late to make those lifestyle changes you've been wanting to make. Unless, of course, you've got a bigger desk than Ben.

We hear Ben gasp for breath in the background as he reaches for that last bag of potato chips. *Gasp, crunch, gasp, crunch.* It's enough to drive anyone to the treadmill.

Health food stores play on our fears, too. They convince us to buy extracts of vegetables we didn't even know existed and make us believe that if pureed and blended together, they're somehow going to taste better. They don't. I'm sorry, but a rutabaga-leek-broccoli-cauliflower swirl is still going to taste pretty much like rutabagas, leeks, broccoli, and cauliflower. A blender and crushed ice isn't going to make them taste like a hot fudge sundae.

But we also know that our bodies need those vitamins, minerals, and, of course, the roughage. The older we get, the more maintenance our bodies require. After forty-plus years, we've had one too many medical tests that show exactly where all that fat we've been consuming over the years has deposited itself. We've seen the ultrasounds, the echocardiograms, the Post-it Notes on our medical reports. We know the blood in our arteries and veins isn't flowing like it did in our youth. We're not fools. Nor are we suicidal. We know if we're going to make it to a ripe old age, we've got to make some changes in our eating habits. We've got to start thinking of that cheesecake as the enemy instead of our reward for doing those three push-ups. We need to start reaching for that bowl of stewed prunes instead of that leaning tower of brownies. And instead of ordering the fried mozzarella sticks, we need to take a second look at those alfalfa sprouts and tofu squares. (Maybe we don't have to go so far as to eat them, but we should at least give them a second look.)

We have to make a commitment to be kinder, gentler to our bodies. We don't want to overwork our hearts or place any unnecessary strain on the rest of our vital organs. One way is to limit our intake of red meat. Cutting out red meat is no problem for me. Most of the meat I serve is black anyway, not red. Including more fish in our diet is a good way to become healthier, too. We should be filling our freezers with rainbow trout, mahimahi, orange roughy, and salmon. They sit nicely on top of the Ben and Jerry's.

You see, there are plenty of ways to improve our eating habits and insure a long, healthy life. But a rutabaga-leek-broccoli-cauliflower swirl? I don't think so. Unless they add a scoop of Rocky Road.

And in the end it's not the years in your life
that count. It's the life in your years.
—Abraham Lincoln

13

I've Only Got Eyelids for You

My good friends Linda Aleahmad, a licensed marriage and family therapist, and Mary Scott, a poet and administrative assistant to a Southern California newspaper editor, and I celebrate our birthdays together each year. We usually go out to a nice restaurant and talk about things like life, work, children, and of course, growing older. No matter how much we don't want to be reminded of it, the subject of aging almost always comes up, and we spend the rest of the evening comparing our latest physical changes and laughing about them as much as possible.

Tonight the physical change du jour was droopy eyelids. Each of us noted that our once perky eyelids had recently unperked themselves, and as Joshua might have said at the wall of Jericho, "They've come a tumbling down!" Not that we're tripping over them or anything, but they've drooped enough to give us that half-open, half-closed look that so many of us had through high school and college.

It seemed to happen to each of us overnight. Eyelids are sneaky that way. You go to bed with all your body parts exactly where they're supposed to be: Chin in place? *Check.* Lips in place? *Check.* Eyelids where they're supposed to be? *Check.* But when you wake up in the morning and look in the mirror, you notice that the rest of your body is exactly where it was eight hours ago, but your eyelids are now drooping like Deputy Dawg's, and you're just about as excited as he is about it.

I suppose we shouldn't be surprised. Our eyelids can't be expected to stay at attention forever. Forty or fifty years is long enough. They're pooped. They're ready for a break. They've faithfully served at their post and now they deserve a rest.

Unfortunately, though, their early retirement begins to place undo pressure on the eyelashes. They are the only things between the avalanche of flesh and our cheekbones.

A business associate of mine had her eyelids pulled back surgically. That's one solution, I suppose. And yes, it worked, but now she has that wide-awake look, like someone just said, "Boo!"

My friends and I spent the evening together weighing the pros and cons of getting our eyelids done but decided against it. We opted to keep the skin we're in and let nature take its course. We would be thankful for our health, our families, and all our blessings. It seemed like the right thing to do—especially when we remembered that Thanksgiving was just around the corner.

I think there was something about my neck that reminded them.

There's more to life than increasing its speed.
—Gandhi

14

Death Doesn't Become Us

Since my friend Mary had recently attended a family funeral, the subject moved from fallen eyelids to funerals, wills, and last wishes. Linda was the first to share what she wanted done with her remains.

"I want to be cremated," she said, "and my ashes placed inside a firecracker and shot into the air in one spectacular send-off."

We figured it must be the cheesecake gone to her head.

Mary said she wanted to be cremated, too, but she also wanted a memorial service in which people said nice things about her. She also wanted a good picture on display, and she'd like her ashes scattered in the barranca in Ventura, California.

I opted for a more traditional funeral. I want nice things said about me at my funeral, too (I'll write them up ahead of time), but I also want the service to be full of funny remembrances. I've embraced laughter my entire life. I wouldn't want it to be missing from my funeral. I want tears, too, of course (who doesn't want to be missed?), but I would hope there'd be lots of laughter to balance things out.

I also asked them to help my husband with the telephone calls. I know him too well. He'll have every intention of calling all my friends listed in our telephone book, but he won't make it past the Cs. It'll be wearying to keep relating the same story over and over again, reliving all the details of how I left this world—especially if I go in some bizarre way like "The manager at the skating rink said it was the first time they'd ever lost anyone during the Hokey Pokey, but they're still going to award her the free CD posthumously for all her efforts." Or "We told her not to use the computer while in the bathtub, but she just mumbled something about a deadline, plugged it in, and deleted herself. We tried to save her as a text file, but we got there too late."

However it happens, my husband will get tired of telling the same tale again and again and again, so he'll just quit— right after the Cs. My friends whose last names begin with the letters *D* through *Z* won't find out about my demise until I'm missing from the family-photo Christmas card. I can hear the phone calls now.

"Where's Martha? I didn't see her by the tree."

"Oh, didn't you know?" my husband will say. "She passed on six months ago."

"Why didn't anyone tell me?"

"I would have, but you weren't in the front of the phone book."

Linda and Mary understood my dilemma (most women can) and agreed to help my husband with the phone calls.

The three of us then moved on to discuss where we wanted our remains to be buried. Living in both Los Angeles and Nashville, I wasn't sure where I'd want my services, so I left the options open. I even entertained the idea of having a service in both places. I didn't see a problem with that, especially since Linda, being shot off in a firecracker, would be having multiple resting places, too. Linda and Mary both opted for California since that's where they live.

Mary wanted the songs "In My Life" by the Beatles and Van Morrison's "Have I Told You Lately That I Love You?" played at her service, and she wanted someone to read several poems, which she has selected. Linda mentioned she wanted "Muskrat Love" sung at hers, but I think she was kidding. I'm still deciding on the songs I want played, but "No One Ever Cared for Me Like Jesus" is definitely one of them.

Next we talked about our choice of flowers. Mary wants irises or tulips. Linda's favorites are daisies and pansies. Mine are magnolias.

We also talked about whether or not we wanted to be organ donors and what parts of our bodies we would be willing to give to science. Not liking the prospect of science returning some of these parts (as defective), we decided not to worry about making these plans right now.

In fact, we decided to change the subject altogether. It was getting way too maudlin. We each felt we had plenty of life left to live, and most of our plans still needed tweaking anyway. Especially Linda's. She wants her funeral in Los Angeles, where fireworks are illegal. That would mean Mary and I would either have to get special clearance or get into a lot of trouble fulfilling her last wishes.

And to tell you the truth, we're not about to get arrested for shooting off a firecracker illegally, even if our best friend is in it.

Despite the high cost of living, it remains a
popular item.
—Anonymous

15

Are We Having Fun Yet?

My husband and I spent last Fourth of July doing laundry at the local all-night Laundromat. What can I say? We're still party animals after all these years.

Actually it was my husband's idea. I was ready to celebrate our nation's birthday like it should be celebrated—an old-fashioned barbecue, picnic games, fireworks, a nap. But no, we had laundry to do.

My husband didn't see any problem with doing our laundry on the Fourth of July. He's of the impression that the older he gets the less holiday excitement he can handle. He prefers nice quiet evenings with the History Channel or curling up with a good book (the Best Buy catalog counts). If my husband had his way, New Year's Eve would be spent getting the transmission fluid checked on our car, Valentine's Day reseeding the lawn, and Christmas morning the perfect time to shampoo the carpets.

His main problem with holidays is he doesn't like crowds. According to him, two's company and three's an unlawful assembly. So since the Fourth of July meant crowds, we did laundry.

Unbeknownst to us, though, the parking lot of the Laundromat happened to be the ideal location for local residents to watch the city's fireworks display. While we were busy fluffing and folding, cars began filing into the parking lot one by one, staking claim on the spaces with the best views. Not that all those people were in for any more excitement than we were going to experience *inside* the Laundromat. Until you've watched a Maytag hit the spin cycle and start shaking in time to "God Bless America" being played over the Laundromat TV, you haven't celebrated the Fourth of July. And if one of the dryers happens to develop an electrical short and the sparks start to fly, well, even Bob Hope would have a hard time beating a finale like that.

So there we were celebrating the Fourth of July in style. No, we wouldn't be seeing the Blue Angels in a flyby (although there were a couple of wasps inside that were putting on quite a show). There wouldn't be a marching band or rockets going off or even sparklers. It was just the two of us with a pocketful of quarters and five loads of laundry needing to be done.

Now that I look back on it, it was a pretty enjoyable evening. We actually got to see some of the fireworks through the reflections in the washing machine portholes, and my husband found a quarter behind one of the chairs. As Yakov Smirnoff would say, "What a country!"

YOU KNOW YOU'RE GETTING OLD WHEN ...
you start buying Geritol by the six-pack.

16

Thanks for the Memory ... Loss

Memory is another thing that dulls with age. But more importantly, memory is another thing that dulls with age. As you grow older, you'll find yourself repeating things and forgetting where you put your glasses, your car keys, your checkbook . . . your teeth. I heard of one older gentleman who looked all over the house for his dentures. He finally found them hours later when he sat down on his sofa. Imagine explaining that one to the emergency room team: *"I don't care if it is physically impossible, doctor, I'm telling you the truth. The bite was self-inflicted."*

We all know the negatives about losing our memory, but believe it or not, there are some positives. For one thing, think of all the new cars you get to drive home.

"Whaddya mean we don't own a Lexus, honey? It was parked in the same parking space I distinctly remember parking in. It's got to be our car!"

One night you get to drive home a Lexus, the next night a Suburban, the next night a BMW convertible. For some reason, though, if you find a Yugo parked in your spot, your memory usually comes back to you.

Another plus to memory loss is the fact that there always seems to be more money in your checkbook than there should be. That's because you don't remember to record amounts written and to whom. I'm still working off the deposits I made six months ago. I think I've spent the same money five or six times. Maybe that's why my bank keeps sending me all those letters . . . and here all this time I thought they were just being neighborly!

There are other good things about losing your memory. When your memory goes, your Christmas list gets cut in half. "How many kids did you say we had again?"

And without a good memory, you only have to mail in your taxes *every other* April 15 or whenever you happen to remember you've got an Uncle Sam. That alone should take some of the sting out of aging.

You even start visiting your neighbors more often. Of

course, it's because you think that's where you live, but they don't know that. They might, however, get a little suspicious when an entire season passes before you say you need to go home.

It hasn't been proven yet, but I'm fairly certain our memory cells die faster with physical exertion. They must. Think about it: How many times have you walked into a room to get something only to stand there looking around wondering what it was you went into the room to get?

I think it's the walking that does it. If you would have stayed in your chair just thinking about getting up to get whatever it was you needed to get up and get, you would have remembered what it was you were going to get up and get in the first place.

Memory cells die off while using the telephone, too. Has this ever happened to you? You dial a number, then completely forget who it is you're calling. You don't hang up, of course, because you're sure you'll remember who you called the minute you hear the voice on the other end of the line. Unfortunately, though, a six-year-old answers, and you're still clueless. The kid doesn't help you out, either, when you ask him who his parents are because he's been taught not to talk to strangers. So you simply pretend to have dialed the wrong number, until the six-year-old finally recognizes *your* voice and says, "Grandpa!"

What I don't get is why our memory has to go on the blink at a time when we're given so much to remember. Our doctors tell us to take three of one pill four times a day, four of another pill three times a day, and one of yet another every ten hours for twelve days. How are we supposed to remember all that? Why can't they just put all our medications into one giant capsule that's set to release the proper dosage at the proper time? Sure, they make those little containers marked Sunday, Monday, Tuesday . . . but what good are they if you don't know what day it is?

Then there are all those other numbers we have to memorize nowadays: our bank account number, our driver's license number, our Social Security number, the PIN numbers for twelve credit cards, our previous three addresses, our age, and our frequent-flyer account numbers. I don't know why we can't be assigned one number for all of it and stay with that for the rest of our lives. Like twenty-five. I'd be happy to keep the number twenty-five for my PIN, my phone card number, and my permanent age.

Long-term memory doesn't seem to be as big a problem as short-term memory. While we may not be able to remember what we said to someone five minutes ago, we can clearly recall the hurtful comment our spouse made back in 1984, what he was wearing at the time, and the barometric pressure that day.

Some people call that selective memory. Maybe it is. Maybe as we grow older we get better and better at selective memory. We remember in vivid detail those few things that brought us pain, while forgetting the hundreds of blessings that come our way every day.

I think we've got it backward.

None are as old as those who have outlived enthusiasm.
—Henry David Thoreau

17

You Don't Bring Me Flowers Anymore

It happens over a period of time, a change so slow you hardly notice it. First, it's your birthday gift. Instead of getting that cute little nightie with the embroidered hearts, you open the gift bag and discover a lovely pair of flannel pajamas, complete with feet. You tell your husband you love them, and to a certain extent, it's true.

You appreciate the fact that the pajamas will keep you warm when he sets the thermostat to twenty degrees (minus-four degrees wind chill factor with the ceiling fan). But flannel pajamas, no matter how well crafted, could mean more than toasty warmth on those chilly summer nights. They could be a warning sign that something has changed in your relationship—not a serious change, just a notable one.

Christmas gifts are affected next. Maybe you get an egg poacher instead of those marcasite earrings you had your heart set on. Or maybe it's an industrial-size container of Spray 'n' Wash instead of the perfume you wanted.

Anniversary presents are the last to change. Instead of pearls, it's plumbing supplies; a makeup kit is replaced with oven cleaner; and that romantic weekend getaway you've been hinting about for months has become a pass for an all-night bowling session.

When these gift changes start to happen in a relationship, there's no denying it—you have a problem. It's called practicality. Now on the surface there's nothing wrong with practicality. After all, why buy your sweetheart a box of chocolates when you really need a new toilet plunger? And with roses costing up to seventy-five dollars a dozen, why waste that kind of money when you can rent a carpet shampooer for half the price?

If we're not careful, by the time we reach middle age the romance in our lives can be virtually nonexistent. We can become too comfortable with our spouse, taking him or her so much for granted that we stop doing those little things that are so necessary to keep love alive. We can easily fall into the trap of never paying attention to our loved ones until they walk in front of the TV while we're watching our favorite show or tie up the telephone when we're expecting a call.

Think about it—when was the last time you went for a walk with your husband? (Helping him take out the garbage doesn't count.) Did the last note you left on the dresser tell him you love him or was it a reminder to pay the electric bill? And husbands, when was the last time you brought your wife flowers, besides that packet of seeds you gave her to plant last spring?

The good news is your romance doesn't have to grow cold. You may not be the young starry-eyed couple you used to be, but you're still a couple. Some of the most romantic couples I've seen are in their seventies and eighties.

There's something wonderful that develops between a man and a woman who have survived all the storms of life together. They can celebrate their fortieth, fiftieth, or even their seventy-fifth wedding anniversary and look back on a *good* marriage—no marriage is perfect—to which they have stayed true. Their disagreements taught them how to compromise, and through their disappointments they learned to appreciate the good times. Instead of growing out of marriage, they persevered and grew in it.

To endure is the first thing a child ought to learn, and that which he will have the most need to know.

—Jean-Jacques Rousseau

18

Regrets

One of my favorite songs is George Burns' "I Wish I Were Eighteen Again." It's the kind of song that makes you feel good and sad at the same time. ("You're the Reason Our Kids Are Ugly" does that, too, but in a different way.)

Whether you've just turned forty or you're nudging one hundred, by now you've no doubt accumulated your share of regrets. When you look back on your life, there are things you'd do differently if you were eighteen again. Or twenty-five. Or thirty. You know the things you wish you had done but didn't and the things you wish you hadn't done but did. There are people you'd like to have spent more time with and a few with whom you might regret having spent so much time. There are places you wish you had visited and a few you might wish you had skipped.

Maybe you regret having taken so many risks. Maybe you wish you had taken more. Now that you see the bigger picture, you wish you hadn't wasted so much time worrying, because what you worried about never came about and the difficulties you did face never could have been imagined.

If you could do it all over again, maybe you'd want to make more money, save more money, or give more away. Maybe you'd have the same friends; maybe you'd choose different ones. You'd surely trust some people more because you can see now that they are trustworthy and you'd trust some people less because of your experience with them. Maybe this time around you wouldn't treat each day as cavalierly as you have in the past.

As much as we'd like to do a better job the second time around, the truth is *this is it*. Whatever regrets we have now are going to go with us into eternity unless we take steps now to change them.

I have regrets I need to deal with.

I regret the time I spent waiting for the other person to call when I had the power to pick up the phone myself.

I regret not verbalizing my opinions instead of verbalizing my frustration with not being able to verbalize my opinions.

I regret not keeping more journals. I had plenty of blank books but usually forgot to write in them. Journals are not meant to remain blank. A blank journal gives the impression you've had a blank life. Nobody leads a blank life. Even if it feels blank some days, it's really not. If you woke up on Wednesday morning, May 14, that's noteworthy. If you didn't wake up, you wouldn't be able to write that in your journal; in fact, it's the only viable excuse for not writing in your journal.

I regret not trying out all the recipes I tore out of magazines. What was I saving them for?

I regret the time I wasted wishing I had more time.

I regret not standing up to the bullies who crossed my path. It takes a lot of courage to confront a bully. That courage never came easy for me.

What I don't regret is the time I've spent with my family and friends. I don't regret anything I've ever done that might in some small way have had an eternal significance in someone else's life. And I don't regret dedicating my life to God at the age of six and the fact that I am still trying my best to honor that commitment today at age . . . well, you know, somewhere over forty.

We make a living by what we get, we make a
life by what we give.
—Winston Churchill

19

The Gravity of the Situation

I doubt if I'll ever forget it. It was one of those images that burn in your memory like a scene from a low-budget horror film. I couldn't sleep for days, and if I've ever been certain of anything, I'm certain of this: I never want to see it again.

It was early in the morning, an ordinary day—nothing much planned except a business meeting I had to attend in about an hour.

I curled my hair with my curling iron just as I do every morning, then began to brush it out. Having read somewhere that brushing your hair upside down gives it more body, I decided to give it a try. Fat hair should be everyone's goal in life, right? So I bent over and brushed . . . and brushed . . . and brushed. I could feel my hair thickening with each stroke. Not being able to resist the temptation, I turned my head to the side and peeked at the mirror. I caught a glimpse of my hefty hair in all of its glory all right, but I also saw something else. I hadn't bargained for this. It was a complete shock. To this day it sends shivers up and down my spine.

What the "Ambassador of Obese Hair" forgot to mention about upside-down brushing was the fact that a woman over the age of forty should never look at herself in the mirror with her head down. If you're over forty and you bend over, all forty years bend with you, believe me. Gravity kicks in, and every fold of skin that has ever thought about becoming a wrinkle suddenly gets its wish. Your hair may look great, but your face looks like Methuselah's mother on her second week without sleep—during allergy season.

This is why when an older movie star is interviewed she tilts her head back in an unnatural position. Notice this the next time you see one on a talk show. Her head is tipped back so far you could give her a sinus exam. No doubt she's had the experience I had the day I bent over and then looked in the mirror. Stephen King may have gotten his inspiration for his last three novels after doing this himself.

I don't recall this phenomenon occurring when I was

younger. I could bend over and tie a shoe, bend over and scratch my leg, bend over and take the dishes out of the dishwasher, and my skin stayed pretty much in place. I'm sure I could look at myself in the mirror upside down or right side up and know beyond a shadow of a doubt who I was.

But the person I saw that day was someone else entirely. Someone who looked about fifty years older and a lot scarier than the right-side-up version. Thus, I've decided to stick with my anorexic hair.

I suppose it has something to do with the law of gravity. Gravity affects our whole body, skin included, and there's not much we can do about it. Areas that used to hold their own now seem to be falling faster than the stock market after an interest hike. Gravity affects men and women alike. It strikes people of every race, creed, and regional setting. You may be a northerner, but by the time you hit middle age, your body will be heading south.

For all its negative effects on the body, though, gravity does have its advantages. For one thing, it's what keeps us from floating off into outer space. And since there aren't any outlet stores on Mars, that's a good thing.

I can't retire. Who'd support my mom and dad?
—George Burns

20

All Grown Up

I distinctly remember the last Christmas my mother gave me a doll. Being a junior-higher, I considered myself much too grown up for dolls. Dolls were for little girls, not young adults. I tried to act pleased but I was more embarrassed than pleased. Couldn't Mom have given me something more appropriate to my age? Something more mature? Something like a nice sweater, a daily planner, or maybe even a pair of high heels?

After all, I had just turned thirteen. *Thirteen*. How much more grown up could I get? It was time for me to put away childish things, to move from Barbie to Bach, or at least to rock. I was growing up and needed grown-up gifts. I didn't play with dolls anymore. I hadn't played with dolls in several weeks, at least. Hadn't Mom noticed that?

I was a young adult. I wanted to be included in adult conversations about news events. I knew who the president of our country was, and I was part of the working class—I had a job babysitting twice a month. I was certain I could hold my own on any adult topic. I had even been watching TV like an adult. No more cartoons except on Saturdays and after school three or four times a week. Instead, I was tuning in to shows like *Meet the Press* and *60 Minutes*. You won't hear a single "Yabba-dabba-do" or "Th-th-that's all, folks!" on either of these award-winning programs. (OK, maybe between takes, but that's different.)

I was dressing like an adult, too. Instead of cut-off jeans and a T-shirt, I was wearing more sophisticated attire—skirts, blouses, and formal T-shirts. I was changing right before Mom's eyes, yet had she picked up on even one of the signals? Apparently not.

So there I was—holding the newly unwrapped doll in my lap and trying desperately to release the words "Thank you" from my lips. When I finally did, it wasn't very convincing.

Don't get me wrong. I realize many perfectly well adjusted adults still have dolls, and that's fine—for them. I have a lot of my dolls on display in my home, too. But at this particular point in my life I was trying desperately to be accepted into the adult world, and Mom's gift set all my efforts back an eternity, or at least a couple of years. All I wanted was to be treated as the intellectual, deep-thinking thirteen-year-old I was so certain I had become.

Mom, on the other hand, was trying her best to hang on to

the child in me. I was the youngest of her five children, her last baby, and the fact that I was growing up meant she was getting older, too. It was a truth she may not have wanted to face—not yet anyway.

None of us can control our own aging process, so we sometimes do what we can to delay the aging process of others. We think if we can just slow the clock for them, our own clock might slow down, too. We do this with TV and movie stars. We don't want to admit they're aging at all. It threatens our own youth. So through the miracle of film and videotape, we trap them in their younger days, before gray hair and gravity set in. And we make them stay there. We place an unfair burden on them to always look young, act young, and sound young, while our own aging process continues unabated.

The simple truth is we're all growing older, even those we so desperately wish wouldn't. So, yes, I forced a smile, said thank you once again, and went to my room. If she didn't want me to grow up, who was I to take that away from her?

Later that evening, after I had sufficiently displayed my dissatisfaction with the doll, at least in the privacy of my room—I took it out of its package and started playing with it. I even had fun.

I guess I didn't really want to grow up so fast, either.

YOU KNOW YOU'RE GETTING OLD WHEN ...

you find yourself wishing recliners had ejection seats.

21

A Hairy Experience

I don't know why, but for some reason, as we grow older we start growing hair in places where hair never grew before. I'm not sure what the medical term for this is, but I'd hazard a guess that the words "Big Foot" are in there somewhere.

I have a hair on my cheek that can grow two inches long if I let it. It's blond, so I can't always see it when I look in the mirror. Most of the time my husband will notice it first.

"If you're going to keep that," he'll say, pointing at the stray hair, "don't you think you oughta perm it?"

He's such a romantic.

There's a hair on my chin that can take a growing spurt, too. I usually don't notice that one until it's curling itself into my bowl of cereal.

I'm not sure why aging makes previously well mannered hair start doing these kinds of strange things, but it does. Maybe it's a hormone thing. Hormones like to act up at this particular time in our lives, so if our ankles start growing side-burns, we shouldn't panic. It might just be a side effect of per-fectly normal hormonal changes.

I am actually having the opposite problem now. For some reason, when I hit thirty-five the hairs on my legs stopped growing altogether. I don't mind, of course. Shaving was always a high-risk ordeal for me. I'd end up with more cuts and slashes than a Republican budget. So who knows, not having to shave my legs may have increased my life expectancy by ten years.

The hair on my head is getting thinner, too. I first noticed something was happening when I was able to fit all of it onto one large curler. And brushing my hair out each morning was taking less and less time. Even my bangs are thinning out. They look like a little blond picket fence that's missing more posts than it started with.

Not only does the volume of our hair change as we get older but also the color. My husband's hair is almost all gray. I've been trying to get him to use a permanent hair color for men, but so far he's holding out. He thinks leaving work on Fri-day with gray hair and returning on Monday with black hair might not be as undetectable as the TV ads imply. He feels he can't explain the younger look as having simply caught up on his sleep.

Another thing that hair starts to do, especially on men, is back up, turn inward, and start to grow out of their ears. Most men don't mind. To them, hair is hair no matter where it grows. Some men even go so far as to grow out their ear hairs and comb them up over their bald spot. I think that's carrying things a bit too far. If it gets that bad, maybe they should just go ahead and shave their whole head. It didn't hurt the careers of Yul Brynner, Telly Savalas, or Michael Jordan.

My father was able to keep a full head of hair into his seventies. The hair on his head stayed put, but he developed a receding eyebrow, forcing him to color it in with an eyebrow pencil. He wasn't happy about it, but he did what he had to do. Well, guess who inherited his unnatural hair loss? I started losing my left eyebrow about a decade ago. Of all the things I could lose, I suppose an eyebrow isn't so bad. At least I can color it in. It's harder to color in a gall bladder.

No matter what color our hair is, whatever unnatural place it's started to grow, or how much of it we have left, the most important thing to remember is this: it doesn't work that well as dental floss, so try to keep it out of your cereal.

He is so old that his blood type was
discontinued.
—Bill Dana

22

A Cut Above

After grocery shopping today, I walked to my car and found an ad for the services of a plastic surgeon tucked under the left windshield wiper. I didn't take it personally. I really doubt that a plastic surgeon was lurking in the bushes waiting for a good candidate to happen along. Yet there it was in black and white—telling me how I could take five, ten, twenty years off my appearance with the mere snip of some surgical scissors.

Now, as tempting as a more youthful look sounded, the word "snip" gave me pause. I don't like that word used in conjunction with one of my body parts. Snip and clip is what we do to hedges, tree limbs, and chicken parts. We even snip and clip our hair, but it doesn't involve anesthesia, bruising, or a four-week recovery period (unless, of course, it's a really bad haircut).

But a lot of people are opting for plastic surgery these days. I guess they're not buying into the notion that wrinkles add character. They're going the snipping, clipping, reshaping, moving-this-here-and-that-there route. They rearrange their faces like some people rearrange their furniture. One thing that gets interesting is their photo Christmas cards. It's almost like going through a family album in reverse.

Plastic surgeons now offer all sorts of new procedures, so no matter what you're unhappy with, they can fix it. They can even lift the whole face, make the necessary adjustments, and reattach it again. A friend of mine had something like this done and the end result was terrific. Even so, it sounds a bit drastic for me. I'd probably get a surgeon with a sense of humor who'd put my face back on upside down to see how long it took for people to notice.

Laser surgery and chemical treatments are getting popular, too. Some of the results can be quite remarkable, but again, I'd be afraid something would go wrong. What if I ended up with a cute little chin cleft right where my nose used to be?

So, after reading the advertisement on my windshield, I tossed it on the passenger's seat and drove home. I knew I'd never call for an appointment, but I thought about calling to offer a good business tip: Leaving flyers on cars parked in grocery store parking lots isn't going to gain a lot of new clients. If this guy really wants his phone ringing off the hook, he needs to place his ad where it will get some attention: the mirrors in ladies' dressing rooms. Everyone knows that when a woman looks at herself in dressing room lighting, she always looks at least twenty years older. We forget all about the outfit we're trying on and gaze in disbelief at the decrepit stranger staring back at us in the mirror. If a plastic surgeon's business card were taped there, we might rush to the nearest pay phone. Better yet, he could move his office to the mall and save us all a lot of time and effort.

Grow old with me. The best is yet to be, the last of life, for which the first was made.

—Robert Browning

23

Old Friends

New jobs, new homes, new churches—all bring the possibilities of making new friends. And making new friends is one of the things that keeps life exciting. But there's something to be said for old friends—friends who have been there through the good and the bad: a wedding, a divorce, the births of our babies, child-rearing, illness, hospital stays, job loss, moving, birthdays, funerals. Friends who've remained close no matter how many miles have come between us. Friends who have stuck by us even when it was difficult to do so.

Some of the following may apply to new friends, too, but they definitely describe old friends.

Old friends know just when to call.
Old friends don't need an excuse to drop by.
Old friends can be trusted with secrets.
Old friends know what you're thinking even before you
   speak.

Old friends aren't jealous of your successes or pleased with your failures.

Even when years have passed, old friends can pick up right where they left off.

A stroll in the park, lunch, or a day of shopping—it doesn't take much to have fun with an old friend.

Old friends don't have to ask, "What can I do to help?" They just know.

Old friends don't only know the real you, they prefer it.

When disagreements arise, old friends don't have to be right.

Old friends overlook your faults instead of keeping a list of them.

Old friends treat you the same behind your back as they do when they are with you.

Old friends give you the benefit of the doubt.

Old friends have stood the test of time, time and time and time again.

Old friends are like antiques—the longer you have them, the more valuable they become.

Old friends are what friendship is all about.

YOU KNOW YOU'RE GETTING OLD WHEN ...

your grandchild asks you to close your eyes so
she can give you a surprise, and you don't wake
up until the following afternoon.

24

Blisters, Sweat, and Tears

Exercise is important at any age, but it's especially important for those of us who are over forty. Lucky for me, there's a fully equipped state-of-the-art YMCA gym about a mile or so from my home. It has everything—rowing machines, exercise bicycles, an Olympic-size swimming pool, aerobics classes. I know this because I drive by it every night on my way to Baskin Robbins. I looked into joining it, but they suggested I wait until they opened their new Intensive Care Unit (I think that's their code name for advanced classes).

Physical exertion has never been high on my priority list, so it's a good thing I became a writer. Producers and editors don't often ask you to "drop and give me two hundred push-ups." (Well, maybe during contract negotiations, but that's all.)

Realizing the importance of exercise, I have managed to work some of it into my daily routine. Whenever possible, I take the stairs instead of the elevator, especially if I'm going down. And now I *run* to the ice cream truck instead of walking to it. It's a good workout and easier to catch up to it that way.

I enjoy bowling, which is good exercise, especially since I prefer to walk down to the pins before releasing the ball. Not only do I burn more calories this way but I also better my score.

Tennis doesn't work as well for me. I find it too difficult to keep track of the ball, and it's much too tempting to use the net as a hammock.

I've tried working out on various forms of exercise equipment, but they're not my cup of sweat, either. The idea of lifting weights doesn't appeal to me in the least. I figure carrying junk mail into the house every day and tossing it into the wastebasket gives my muscles all the workout they need.

My experience with a treadmill was less than beneficial. I had one for a while, and my cardiovascular system might have gotten a good workout on it, but my pillow kept getting stuck on the conveyor belt.

Since I don't like traditional forms of exercise, someone

once asked me if I'd ever thought about giving clogging a try. Other than my arteries, I had to say no. Clogging does appear to be a great workout, though, so I've ordered a couple of video-tapes to learn how to do it. I figure if it doesn't get me into shape, at least it'd be a fun way to strip the varnish from my hardwood floors.

Walking is still one of the safest and most effective forms of exercise for those of us over forty, so I try to do a little each day. My favorite place to walk is the airport. If you've never tried it, you should check it out sometime. It's air-conditioned, you get to meet a lot of different people from all over the world, and if you walk on the moving sidewalks, you can do two miles in nothing flat.

Even though I don't exhibit much energy on the outside, in my mind I'm a workout fool. There's absolutely no exercise I can't picture myself doing. Mention aerobics, and in my mind I'm Jane Fonda. Gymnastics? I'm Mary Lou Retton. Swimming? I'm one of the lifeguards on *Baywatch*. But that's just in my head. In reality, I'm more like Aunt Bea, Grandma Moses, and one of the near-drowning victims on *Baywatch*.

One of the reasons I don't exercise is because of a bad expe-rience I once had. Someone told me a vibrator belt was good for shaking your body into shape. You just wrap it around yourself, turn it on, and let it shake you like a bowl of Jell-O. It sounded simple enough. Besides, they also said it would help get rid of my cellulite, so I decided to give it a try. I used it on my hips and my legs, and when they suggested I try it on my arms, I gave those a good shaking, too. It worked, but not in the way I had imagined.

When I woke up the next morning, I looked in the mirror and noticed something odd, something very different from the firm image I expected. For some reason, all my upper arm fat had slid down to my elbows. There were huge indentations in my upper arms—sinkholes, if you will—that dipped almost to the bone. I had fat-free upper arms and elbows the size of swim floats. In short, I looked like Popeye. The cellulite didn't go away, it just went south for the winter.

I made an appointment with Dr. Robert Rood, my longtime physician, who after a thorough examination explained that it was some sort of medical oddity. People have used vibrator belts for years, and he had never seen anything like this.

After two years of stares, questions from curious people, and, of course, the Popeye references, I awoke one morning to discover that my upper arm fat had mysteriously returned to where it came from. It had been two long years, but now the fat was back in its rightful place, along with the cellulite, but this time I decided to leave well enough alone.

The rest of my body could still use some work, though.

And since I'm in my forties, I figure it's time to make those changes. It's time to develop an exercise program and stick with it. It's time to . . . I'll get back to this later. I think I just heard the ice cream truck.

You are never too old to set another goal or to
dream a new dream.
—Les Brown

25

You're So Vein

My varicose veins are starting to spell out my name. Not my whole name, of course, just my initials. The M is pretty easy to make out, and right now the B looks more like a P, but it's well on its way. I'm just waiting for the people from *Ripley's Believe It or Not!* to contact me, and I'll be rolling in the dough. Unless, of course, someone else has already beat me to it.

A lot of people over forty have varicose veins. Some even have what they call "spider veins"—the network of veins that look a lot like a spider web. I don't have spider veins yet. I guess God figures I have enough webs around my house to deal with—why make me wear them, too?

My mother had varicose veins. I'm sure there was a medical reason for them, but I personally attributed her condition to the fact that she worked at a department store and was on her feet most of the day. It doesn't seem fair, does it? Hard work should result in a strong heart, good muscle tone, and healthy lungs, not the alphabet suddenly appearing on your calves.

Today there are various treatments for varicose veins, some simple, others more extensive. So far, I think I'll keep mine. They don't actually hurt, and, lucky for me, the blue stripes only clash with a few of my outfits.

I've got so many liver spots I should come
with a side of onions.
—Phyllis Diller

26

Where's Your Drive?

I don't believe age should be a determining factor in issuing a driver's license. One's driving skill, reflexes, and knowledge of the highway laws are what should be held up to scrutiny. Age is nothing more than a number.

At the age of seventy, my mother scored 100 percent on her driving test. She was an excellent driver who preferred to drive in the slow lane whenever possible. When making left turns, her motto was "If you wait long enough, it'll eventually be clear." Having to drive the streets of Los Angeles, this motto often kept us waiting at intersections into the night, but Mother was emphatic. Whenever risk could be avoided, she avoided it.

The rules of the road have changed so much lately, I wonder if she'd even pass the test today, much less get another perfect score. Remember the good ol' days when the potential answers to a question like "What do you do when someone is tailgating you?" used to be: (a) slow down, (b) swerve to avoid his hitting you, or (c) gently honk your horn? There wasn't any (d) draw a gun on him, or (e) pull over and beat him to a pulp.

The test is more difficult because of so many societal changes, but as I said, age shouldn't be a determining factor in driver's license renewal. If, however, any of the following apply to you, you might want to consider voluntarily surrendering yours.

IT MIGHT BE TIME TO GIVE UP YOUR DRIVER'S LICENSE IF . . .

- you've ever waited in an intersection through three or more light changes before making your left turn;

- you consider the raised median your personal driving lane;

- you've ever worn out a new brake light on a two-mile trip to the store;

- you refer to going thirty-five miles per hour as "flooring it";

- you've ever honked at a pedestrian and said the words, "Move it, buddy! You think you own the sidewalk?";

- a tractor has passed you on the freeway, and it was being pushed;

- you've ever used a stoplight to get in a short nap;

- you've ever made more than three U-turns within a single block;
- you've driven for more than twenty-five miles with your left turn signal on;
- you've ever tried to report a fire truck for tailgating you.

You're only as old as you feel . . . and I don't feel anything until noon. Then it's time for my nap.

—Bob Hope

27

Beside Myself

I don't like the idea of my skin cells dying every day. I suppose it's perfectly natural; it happens to everybody. We do grow new ones, but it still seems a bit morbid.

What is it that's killing them off anyway? Are they looking at themselves in the mirror every morning and committing suicide? (If you saw how I looked in the morning, you might not blame them.) Whatever it is that's making them die off, shouldn't we be doing something about it? Oh, I realize there are facial masks, skin cleansers, astringents, and all sorts of other skin care products on the market that supposedly do a good job of removing dead skin cells, but I'm talking about something a bit more organized.

Perhaps we could hold fund-raisers or weekend telethons. After all, this is a problem affecting the entire human race. I know I'd rather not have to worry about thousands of cells falling off my body every day and forming a microscopic pile at my feet. If I could save one skin cell from an untimely death, it would be worth whatever work it took to achieve that goal.

But it's hard getting others to feel equally passionate about my cause. All they want to do is scrub dead cells off and let them slide down the drain rather than do anything to save them. I once knew a lady who got so into scrubbing dead cells from her face, she actually drew blood. Obviously she went a bit overboard. She probably took out some cells that were merely in critical condition. I'm sure her intentions were good, but someone needed to tell her there's nothing attractive about raw flesh.

Skin is a good thing. It helps people recognize us, and it keeps the dust out of our vital organs. Even as I'm writing this, though, my own skin cells are continuing to die despite all my efforts to intervene.

I suppose one day they'll try cloning new human beings from dead skin cells. Scientists have already taken the DNA of sheep and cloned exact replicas. Not that I'm saying it's the morally correct thing to do, but there has been a lot of experimentation going on lately. I don't know about you, but I wouldn't want an exact replica of me walking around, especially one that looks younger than I do! And who's to say the clone wouldn't start charging up all my credit cards? Or worse yet, charging *less* than I do? My husband might want to trade me in for the cheaper model.

No matter how much a clone may look like us, though, it can never actually *be* us. For one thing, it wouldn't have our life experiences, and knowing what we do, we'd want to save it from every difficult situation it might have to face. But it's the unique combination of both the difficult times and the happy times in our lives that have made us who we are. So instead of having another "you" running around, all you'd get in a clone is a shallow look-alike.

That's why if my skin cells have to die I'd rather they stay dead. I hate to lose them, but they did their tour of duty. They were faithful to a point, and now it's time for them to say their farewells and go to that big loofah sponge in the sky.

Age should not have its face lifted, but it should
rather teach the world to admire wrinkles as the
etchings of experience and the firm
line of character.
—Ralph B. Perry

28

Happy Birthday to Me

Birthday parties are fun, but they remind us that . . . well, you know—we're getting older. Most of us loved celebrating our birthdays when we were two, eight, sixteen, and even twenty-one. But when we get past forty, we might not want to be re-minded of the number of years we've lived.

Surprise birthday parties can be deadly the older you get. Imagine poor Grandpa walking into the kitchen on the evening of his ninety-ninth birthday. All he wants is that slice of apple pie he's had his eye on all week. He doesn't suspect a thing, and with his impaired eyesight, he certainly can't see the shadows of eighteen people hiding under the counter. He feels along the wall, turns the lights on, and all of a sudden hears, "Surprise!!" The rest of the story can be read in the coroner's report.

Then there are the gifts. Ah, the gifts. After forty, you no longer receive gifts that you really want. Unbeknownst to you, you've suddenly crossed over into a different realm, you've entered into what is known as *The Medical Gift Zone*. You're getting things like medical dictionaries, callous removers, and baskets filled with an assortment of Bengay products.

I suppose to a certain extent it's understandable. After all, nothing says "I love you" like a blood pressure cuff or one of those new at-home cholesterol tests.

When my husband turned forty, the only thing he wanted for his birthday was a full body scan. He didn't have a single symptom, but if something was getting ready to go haywire, he didn't want to be the last to know about it. His reasoning was this: What good is a new power tool if your triglycerides are on a roller coaster ride? A new tie means nothing to someone whose thyroid gland is about to poop out.

A full body scan was what he wanted, and it was my duty as a wife to get it for him. But you can't just go to aisle 14 at Kroger's and pick up one. And if you go to a hospital to buy one, they'll tell you you need a doctor's order.

So I got him a tie . . . and a doctor's appointment. I do want to keep him around for a lot more years. I want to be able to watch him blow out seventy, eighty, or even ninety candles.

It's funny, isn't it? The older we get, the more candles we're expected to blow out. If you ask me, it should be turned around. At our first birthday party, there should be eighty candles to blow out. We've got breath then. We're full of energy and should be able to handle it without having oxygen on standby. Then we could start removing the candles, one per year. That way, by the time we reach eighty we'd have only one candle left to blow out. And if that's too much, we could call in a tag team.

Live your life and forget your age.
—Norman Vincent Peale

29

The Good Ol' Days

If you've lived more than forty years, chances are you've seen a lot of changes. In my lifetime I've seen the advent of the personal computer, the information highway, e-mail, the fax machine, the cell phone, space travel, and pet rocks.

I've seen changes in clothing, too. I've watched bell-bottoms come into style, go out of style, and come back in again. I've seen torn and holey jeans graduate from being a financial statement to a fashion one. I've seen hemlines go up, down, and even shred themselves.

I've seen hairstyles go from long to short to blue to purple to spiked to bald. And that's just the women.

Body piercing used to be something you only saw in *National Geographic* or when you accidentally pierced yourself putting on a new shirt before taking out all the straight pins. Now some people are piercing every body part they can think of. I don't get it. I had two amniocenteses done while pregnant with my last child, and that was all the body piercing I needed for a lifetime.

I've witnessed a lot of changes on the political scene, too. I've seen a president impeached, a president resign, a president assassinated, and one lose his meal in a dignitary's lap at an overseas state dinner.

We've traveled to the moon and had plenty of public figures we'd like to send there.

I've watched dissatisfied, unfulfilled stay-at-home moms join the work force and dissatisfied career women quit their jobs to become stay-at-home moms.

I've seen dads become Mr. Moms when they realized that their children are only young once.

I've seen good changes and some that weren't so good. Changes we've fought against and plenty we've had to learn to accept. But if life is about anything, it's about change. We don't have a choice in that. We do, however, have a choice as to how much *we* change with it.

In three words I can sum up everything I've learned about life: It goes on.

—Robert Frost

30

Extra! Extra!

I've stopped reading the newspaper. Not all of it. Just certain parts of it. OK, just *one* part of it—the "obit" column, otherwise known as the obituaries. Most of the news ruins my day anyway, but the obituary column can ruin it the fastest.

The problem is this: instead of reading the deceased's name, accomplishments, and who they are survived by, my eyes are immediately drawn to their age. I can't help it.

I've talked to other people who do the same thing. If the age of the deceased is anywhere near our own age, give or take twenty years, we spend the rest of the day wondering what it was that took the person. If the poor guy walked in front of a bus and was run over, then we'll be more careful the next time we cross the street, but we won't lose sleep over it. If he slipped at the grocery store, slid into a giant pyramid of canned pinto beans, and was hit square in the temple with the jumbo-sized one, causing a massive brain hemorrhage, we'll feel bad and probably skip that aisle the next time we go grocery shopping, but we're not going to become paranoid over it.

But if they're dropping like flies from things that could easily strike us, too, then we start to worry. That pain in our back suddenly becomes cancer instead of the muscle strain the doctor told us it was. The discomfort in our chest that comes right after eating that fifth slice of sausage, onion, and bell pepper pizza becomes the heart attack we're sure is going to take us. Don't get me wrong. Any persistent symptom should be checked out by your physician, but sometimes we write ourselves off when we've still got plenty of life left.

Personally, I don't want to go until I'm 110. It sounds like the perfect age to leave this world. You've seen it all. You've had fun. It's time to move on. No one talks about a 110-year-old man or woman being "struck down in the prime of life." You won't hear phrases like "It was so sudden. Nobody saw it coming." At 110, everyone sees it coming. You're wearing a sweatshirt that says, "Life—Been There, Done That." You're probably on your third heart and fourth kidney by then.

But the majority of those listed in the obituary column aren't over 100. Most of them are substantially younger than that. That's why I've quit reading it.

One obituary recently caught my eye, though. It was that of Sarah Knauss, who died on December 30, 1999, at the tender young age of 119. Her daughter, Kathryn Sullivan, ninety-six, attributed her mother's longevity to the fact that she was a tranquil person. Nothing could faze her.

So maybe that's the secret to longevity. That and a good sense of humor. George Burns, who also made it past his 100th birthday, used to say that every morning he'd get up and read the obituary column. If his name wasn't there, he'd make breakfast.

According to the U.S. Census Bureau, by the year 2050 the number of people over the age of 100 will be nearly 834,000. That's pretty encouraging. Just imagine all the things you could do if you lived to be over 100 years of age. You could wait until you're fifty to get married and still live long enough to celebrate your golden wedding anniversary (that is, if your spouse lived that long, too). You could put off college until your forties, then get your doctorate and still put in a fifty-year career. You could attend your eightieth high school reunion and take any seat you wanted. You'd probably have to dance by yourself, and your class photo might be of you and the waiter, but you could still have a great time.

Do you realize that at 100 years of age, you could conceivably see the birth of your great-great-great-great-grandchild? What kind of gift do you buy a great-great-great-great-grandchild?

By the time you reach 100, you could have cashed in three consecutive thirty-year bonds and paid off three thirty-year mortgages.

If you live to be 100, chances are you've outlived your parents, your siblings, your doctors, most of your friends, and a lot of your enemies. Your diary would read like a history book, and you wouldn't have any elders to look up to except God.

So if you're lucky enough to live as long as Sarah, or even George, don't just sit there reading the obituary column every morning, wondering whether or not you should get up and make breakfast. Put on your in-line skates and roll on down to the Waffle House.

If I had my life to live over again, I wouldn't
have the time.
—Bob Hope

31

Aka Doughgirl

Lately my cheeks have been looking puffy. I look like the CBS eye—with hair. I don't know why I'm filling out this way. The fact that I've gained fifteen pounds could have something to do with it, I suppose, but I'm not a doctor.

Maybe I got bit by something. Insect bites can make you swell. Or maybe it's an allergic reaction. I could have been allergic to that box of Krispy Kreme donuts I ate the other night.

The thing I don't understand about weight gain is why it takes place in just one or two parts of your anatomy. For some people, it's the hips; for others, it's the stomach; for me, it's the cheeks . . . What's going on? Do all our fat cells gather together in one place and hold meetings? Do they send messages to each other like "Union meeting today, right hip, two o'clock. Be there"? I'm pretty sure my fat cells held a meeting there last week while I was busy eating at an all-you-can-eat buffet. After that third plate, I glanced down at my right hip and it looked like a 100 percent turnout! In fact, it looked like they might have been holding a regional convention.

The way my cheeks have puffed up, I have a feeling they're gathering for the Million Man Fat Cell March. But why my cheeks? If they really felt the need to congregate somewhere, why didn't they go where my body could use some added cells? I have a few suggestions, and I'd be more than happy to direct them there, but so far I haven't been able to figure out how to crash one of their meetings.

In the meantime, if CBS ever needs a double for its logo, they know where to find me.

Life is a great big canvas, and you should throw
all the paint on it you can.
—Danny Kaye

32

Impatiently Ever After

We don't only lose hair and teeth as we grow older, many of us start losing our patience. We just don't put up with as much as we used to. That's why you hear about so many "grouchy old men" or "cranky old ladies." By the time you're sixty or seventy years old, you've had enough. You don't always know what it is you've had enough of, you just know you've had enough of it.

Traffic jams never used to bother me. Now I find myself wishing I had multiple personalities so I could at least drive in the carpool lane.

Slow food service didn't affect me either. But lately I've noticed when my husband takes me to our favorite romantic restaurant, I start honking the minute I don't think their drive-thru lane is moving fast enough.

Perhaps you can identify with what I'm saying. When you're

reading *Snow White and the Seven Dwarfs* for the fourth time to your grandchild, do you find yourself editing the story down to *Snow White and the Four Dwarfs* just to get it over with sooner? Have you been making Cinderella leave the ball by ten o'clock just because *you* can't stay awake until midnight? Has Little Red Riding Hood had to take a taxi to grandmother's house rather than waste time walking through the forest?

If the answer is yes to any of the above, your patience level has reached the danger zone. You can help yourself by (1) buying shorter books to read to your grandchildren, and (2) avoiding things that could possibly make your blood pressure rise. These include but are not limited to . . .

- political campaign speeches;
- people who never put their cell phone down;
- telemarketer calls during dinner;
- broken postage stamp machines;
- businesses that refuse to put you through to a live person no matter how many buttons you press;
- dogs who perform barking concerts at two in the morning;
- closed-minded people who refuse to agree with you no matter how many times you tell them you're right;
- people you let cut in front of you who are so impressed

with your kindness they let twelve people cut in front of them, too;

- door-to-door salesmen who spend more time on your porch than the family cat;
- relatives or friends who only seem to remember your phone number when they need a favor.

The list of things that cause us to lose our patience continues to grow with each passing year. But there are a few things left that most of us can still be patient about. For one thing, I don't have any problem with my dentist taking as long as he needs before calling my name—I could wait for hours and never complain. I'm never in a hurry for April 15 to roll around either. And those February deferred credit card statements? They could arrive in August and you wouldn't hear a peep out of me.

So you see, impatience doesn't have to be an inevitable result of aging. It's up to us whether or not we slow down and enjoy life to the fullest. The sun is going to continue to rise and set at the same speed every day no matter what. So relax and enjoy.

I love long walks, especially when taken by
people who annoy me.
—Fred Allen

33

Life of the Party

I used to be the life of the party at amusement parks. I don't know what happened, but I'm no fun anymore. I know this because everyone else brings home souvenir pictures of themselves on the newest roller coaster ride, right in the middle of the upside-down triple loop. I bring home souvenir pictures of me on one of the stationary animals on the carousel.

It's not that I don't want to ride the roller coaster. I do. I used to ride all those wild rides, but the older I get, the more safety-minded I've become. You can get hurt on a roller coaster, for heaven's sake. Sure, millions ride them every day, and there have been only a few incidences of a person falling out, but it could happen. If I'm riding the roller coaster, I really don't want to end up in the sky buckets. You have a much better time when you get off the same ride you got on.

My day at an amusement park usually goes something like this:

9:00 A.M.—Arrive at park. Discuss renting locker. Everyone convinces me we don't need one.

9:15 A.M.—Buy tickets.

9:30 A.M.—Restroom break

9:40 A.M.—Pass on virtual reality ride. Afraid shaking
might throw my back out.

9:55 A.M.—Walk by log ride. Decide to pass. Getting wet
could give me a chill. Hold jackets and cameras of family and friends (the same ones who
said we didn't need a locker) while they go on
log ride.

10:33 A.M.—Snack break

11:05 A.M.—Walk by roller coaster. Hold jackets, cameras,
and cups of soda of family and friends while
they ride roller coaster.

11:58 A.M.—Lunch break

12:48 P.M.—Ride train after conductor guarantees in writing that the ride only moves in a forward direction and absolutely no water is involved.

1:36 P.M.—Restroom break

2:00 P.M.—Stop at souvenir store. Insert quarter and use
the electric foot massage machine. Get a little
dizzy, but it's worth it.

3:05 P.M.—Walk by spinning teacups. Pass on spinning
teacups (I forgot my Dramamine). Hold jackets, cameras, cups of soda, and bags of souve-

nirs of family and friends while they ride spinning teacups.

3:45 P.M.—Restroom break

4:00 P.M.—See stage show. Try to convince family and friends that it should count as a ride since a slight aftershock hit while we were there, but they don't buy it.

6:10 P.M.—Dinner break

7:35 P.M.—Ride bumper cars

7:45 P.M.—Still trying to figure out how to get my car to move.

8:11 P.M.—Restroom break

8:25 P.M.—Hold jackets, cameras, souvenirs, and doggie bags of friends and family while they ride dinosaur ride. I pass on the ride. (I watched *Jurassic Park* one too many times.)

9:30 P.M.—Walk by lockers on our way back to the car. Family and friends remind me how smart we were to not waste our fifty cents on a locker.

10:45 P.M.—Arrive home. Sit in vibrating recliner. It's exhilarating, free, and I didn't even have to wait in line for it.

To err is human. To forgive is simply
not our policy.
—Source unknown

34

Is There a Doctor in the House?

There's nothing that'll make a person feel older than having to deal with a young professional. The older we get, the younger pilots, police officers, lawyers, and doctors look. Especially doctors. I don't know about you, but I feel uncomfortable going to a doctor who has a Scooby Doo sticker on his residency certificate.

But regardless of how young he looks, we still see him regularly. Why is this? Because medical care is important to us. It's important at any age, but it's especially important as we get older. We're hoping to hold up, but just as a car needs repairs and replacement parts as it ages, so do our bodies. We could be chugging along fine on our factory-installed original equipment, but after those first one hundred thousand miles or so, things could start to go haywire. Our battery doesn't charge like it used to, our fan belt gets a little frayed, and we might even discover a crack in our engine block. And if that's not bad enough, we can develop an embarrassing leak in our transmission. We need help, maybe even a complete overhaul.

Fortunately, I've only had a few things go wrong with my engine over the years. I've had a couple of benign breast cysts removed, some laser surgeries performed on my eyes, and my pancreas needs a little help to work properly. Other than that, I haven't had to spend too much time in the pit, and for that I'm thankful.

But since ours is the age when things can start to go wrong, good health insurance is important. If you don't have private insurance, chances are you have an HMO. I've had both. One thing I've learned about HMOs is that they aren't all the same. Some are terrific and are equipped to meet whatever medical need might arise. Others fall short of the mark.

To aid you in your search for a good HMO, the following list is provided:

YOU KNOW YOU'VE JOINED A CHEAP HMO WHEN . . .

- Resetting a bone involves duct tape.

- For a second opinion, they refer you to last week's episode of *ER*.

- Their EKG machine bears a striking resemblance to an Etch A Sketch.

- Their IV solution looks an awful lot like Kool-Aid.

- They get their X rays developed at Walgreen's.

- They recycle their tongue depressors.

- You get a discount if you make up your own hospital bed.

- Their ambulance rents itself out as an airport shuttle on the off-hours.

- Their thermometer reads to 400 degrees and tastes an awful lot like turkey.

- Their mammogram machine doubles as the waffle iron in the hospital cafeteria.

All the flowers of all the tomorrows are in
the seeds of today.
—Source unknown

35

It's All in the Attitude

Getting older is beyond our control. No matter how much we'd like to, we can't stop time from marching on. However, *growing old* is something we can control. That's where attitude enters in.

When we look in the mirror, we can either see a life that's half over or a life that's half begun. We can spend all our time dwelling on the mistakes of our past or we can spend it focused on the hope of the future. We can count our wrinkles or count our blessings. The choice is ours.

It's been said that we live the first half of our life for success and the second half for significance. I agree. In our twenties and thirties, most of us were consumed with our careers, attaining financial stability, and perhaps raising a family.

By the time we reach the second half of our life, our priorities change—or at least they should. Many of us have had to watch our parents' health decline or fail. At this juncture, we are forced to face the cruel reality that our time on this earth is limited. When we fully realize this, the reports and meetings that seemed so important and pressing suddenly lose their urgency. We spend less time thinking about the mortgage on our home and more about the people in it.

When I was driving my mother to her chemotherapy treatments, she would often remark about the flowers along the side of the road. She noticed them as if for the first time. Of course, she'd driven that road many times before, and the flowers were there each spring, but she wasn't looking at them then. She was usually on her way to work and had a host of other things on her mind. Now, battling cancer, she appreciated their beauty to the fullest.

The second half of life is a chance to get our priorities straight. It's a time to realize that having the last word isn't as important as having a conversation. It's time to quit trying so hard to get ahead of the Joneses and to try a little harder to walk beside them and be their friends. It's time to realize that it's not going to matter how much money you leave your family when you die. What is important is how much of yourself you leave with them.

By the time you're eighty years old, you've
learned everything. You only have to
remember it.
—George Burns

36

I'm My Own Grandma

There's an old country song titled "I'm My Own Grandpa." If my memory serves me correctly, it's about a man whose relatives have married people they're already related to by law—in-laws, stepparents, step-siblings, etc., eventually making him his own legal grandfather.

Now, while the story in the song may be highly unlikely, there's another way to become one's own grandfather, grandmother, mother, or father. Just live long enough.

They say as we grow older, we begin to look and act like those who've gone on before. My sister, Melva, is becoming my mother right before my eyes. Not only does she look like her, she has her expressions and even sounds like her. I wish she would have sounded like her years ago when I was in high school, then when my teachers called the house, they could have talked to Melva instead of Mom and I wouldn't have gotten grounded so often.

One of my mother's favorite sayings was "Food takes the place of sleep." There's absolutely no official documentation to this, but Mom said it as though it were the latest finding of the American Medical Association. She honestly believed that if you had to work late, a meal was as good as a nap. (Maybe that's why I gained those fifteen pounds.)

My sister says things like that now. She reacts to situations as Mother would have, is a hard worker, and has a heart for others. She may not be her own grandpa, but in so many ways she has become her own mother.

I don't remember seeing my mother in my sister in her younger years. When my sister was a teenager, she was just Melva. Even in her twenties she was Melva. She didn't start turning into Mom until recently. The forties seem to be about the time this phenomenon hits. We're going along fine, being our own person, and then one day we look in the mirror and are suddenly struck with the image of one of our parents staring back at us.

I have some of the characteristics of both my parents. I've already mentioned that I inherited my father's eyebrows, but I also have his sense of humor. I have my mom's appreciation for a good joke, her smile—slightly tilted to one side—and I have her almond-shaped blue eyes. Both of my parents were tall with high cheekbones, and I've inherited those qualities, as well. But the person I believe I'm starting to look like the most is my maternal grandmother. I have a picture of her over our bed, and the resemblance between the two of us is becoming more apparent with each passing day.

When you get down to it, we're all a combination of all our ancestors. We might have our father's nose, our mother's eyes, our grandmother's ears, and our great-grandfather's chin. Depending on our family, this could be a good or a bad combination. Yet no matter what physical characteristics we've been blessed with, or stuck with, our inner qualities are what are most important. In other words, heirs should be more grateful for the good judgment they inherited from their father, the gentle spirit they got from their mother, the sense of fairness that was passed down from their grandfather, and the self-esteem imparted to them from their grandmother than they are for whatever physical characteristics they may have inherited.

For the things which are seen are temporal, but the things which are not seen are eternal.
—2 Corinthians 4:18 KJV

37

When You've Got It, You've Got It

I couldn't believe the nerve of this guy. Had he no manners?
Didn't he realize his Neanderthal behavior wasn't appreciated in
the least? Did he not know he was being obnoxious and making a scene? Couldn't he see that I had a cell phone and could
call 9–1–1 at a moment's notice?

Perhaps I should start at the beginning. It happened at the
post office near my house. I had driven there to mail a letter,
and as soon as I got out of my car, he started howling and making wolf calls at me. They were loud, they were rude, and they
were annoying.

I walked to the post office entrance, trying my best to

ignore his junior high behavior, but it was becoming increasingly more difficult.

"Grrrowwwooofff!" he howled loud enough for anyone within a two-block radius to hear. "Grrrowwwooofff! Grrrowwwooofff!" The guy was pathetic.

Finally, I'd just had it. I was ready to give him a piece of my mind or at least shoot him a look that said exactly what that piece of my mind was thinking. But when I turned to glare in his direction, I saw something totally unexpected. That howling wasn't coming from a man. It was coming from a dog—a very large dog upset about being left in a very small car.

I was laughing so hard at myself when I stepped into the post office, the clerks must have thought they had another crazed lunatic on their hands. But I couldn't help it. Here I had thought I was attracting the unwanted advances of a man, when I was merely attracting the attention of a canine who only wanted his freedom. No wonder they say it's not a good idea to jump to conclusions. How we interpret a situation might have very little to do with reality.

So now when I hear someone make some sort of verbal advance at me, I turn to look before I start judging. After all, the next whistle I hear might be coming from a parrot, and it's not easy to press harassment charges against fowl.

YOU KNOW YOU'RE GETTING OLD WHEN ...

you need a running start to go for a walk.

38

Plenty to Smile About

The ad read, "Do your teeth make you look ten years older than you really are?" Now, *there's* a side effect of aging I hadn't even considered.

The advertisement went on to say that as we age our teeth can darken, our gums recede, and our breath start smelling like last week's laundry. I guess wrinkles and age spots weren't enough, now our teeth have to get into the act.

And what's this about receding gums? Why would they want to do a thing like that? There's nothing honorable in receding. Can't they hold on for another twenty or thirty years and then retreat?

None of it seems quite fair, does it? After all the attention we've given our teeth all these years, when we need them most, they're going to start jumping ship one by one.

From as far back as I can remember, my father wore a full set of dentures. I know this because whenever he sneezed they'd fly out of his mouth and land some ten feet away. I don't know if there's ever been an Olympic event for this, but if there were, he would have taken home the gold.

My father even made his own denture repairs. If they didn't fit just right (which was obvious since they were on the frequent-flyer program), he'd heat them over the kitchen stove, remolding them to whatever size or shape was needed. My father was creative that way. He probably could have set up a business fixing dentures for other people, but we lived in a residential area and I doubt if he could have gotten a zoning permit.

But Dad's philosophy was why pay for dental work when you could just as easily do it yourself? Luckily, he didn't have the same attitude when he had to have his appendix removed. I don't think our butter knives could have done the job.

I'm not sure if I'd like having to wear dentures. There's something about putting your teeth in a glass at night and waking up to their smiling back at you that's unsettling. It's a little Stephen King-ish, if you know what I mean.

Darkening teeth and receding gums aren't the only mouth problems we have to be concerned about as we grow older. Over the years my jaw has developed a malady known as TMJ. Because of this condition, my jaw makes a popping sound whenever I eat. Sometimes the popping is so loud a seven-course meal can sound like a reggae concert. One of these days I might look into getting my jaw fixed, but until then I'm still looking to land a recording contract.

We should never allow ourselves to fall into the trap of thinking we're too old to correct mouth or dental problems, however. Some people in their forties or fifties are getting braces for the first time. They're correcting something that has bothered them for years. Too often by the time we reach middle age we tell ourselves, why bother? We figure if we've put up with something this long, why not put up with it for the rest of our lives? That's limited thinking. No matter how old we are, chances are we still have some good years left, so why settle for dingy teeth, receding gums, or loose-fitting dentures?

We should all do what we can to improve our smiles. After all, it's one of the most important aspects of our appearance.

Do not worry, saying, "What shall we eat?" or
"What shall we drink?" or "What shall we
wear?" . . . your heavenly Father knows that
you need them.
—Matthew 6:31–32 NIV

39

Seasons

Growing up in the Los Angeles area, I didn't really get to experience the changes of seasons. The only variation we had was going from wearing long sleeves in winter to short sleeves in spring to no sleeves in summer to three-quarter sleeves in the fall. The only big changes in our weather reports were the jokes.

When I moved to Tennessee, I finally got to see what a real change of seasons looks like. It snows in Tennessee—just enough to remind you that the white stuff exists. After a few months the winter cold gives way to spring with all the dogwoods blooming in bright splashes of pink and white. Summer has a different kind of beauty, with more shades of green than you could imagine. To me, the most beautiful of all seasons here is the fall. I think no matter where I might live in the future, I'd always want to spend some of the fall in Tennessee. The drive from Nashville to the Smoky Mountains is breathtaking. It's as though someone came along and aerial-sprayed barrels of orange, yellow, red, and brown paint all over the countryside.

Being over forty is like being in the fall of your life.

Spring, of course, is the time when new life is birthed, and one can't help but be filled with anticipation for what each new day will bring. It's a period of firsts: the first smile, the first tooth, the first steps, and the first time to shave the cat. A few bruises are earned learning to walk, words are jumbled learning to talk, and a few plates of spaghetti are dumped learning to eat, but eventually these tasks are mastered and one moves on.

The summer of life—the teenage–young adult years—is full of fun and wonder. You experience life on a new level, making your own decisions and having to live with the outcomes. Life is an adventure, and you want to enjoy every minute of it. You might stumble once in a while getting your footing, but you've been around long enough to realize the importance of getting up and trying again.

Fall is the season of change—in nature and in life. Your children are moving out and going away to college or getting married and having children of their own. You might be changing jobs or retiring, downsizing your home, reevaluating your priorities, and altering your opinions on a thing or two. Age tends to mellow all but the most closed-minded individual.

Winter is a time for reflection, a time to look back and smile about the good times and assess what you've learned from the not-so-good times. A tree doesn't fear when winter's coming. It doesn't lower its head and cry because most of its leaves have dried up and fallen off. (OK, maybe a weeping willow cries in winter, but it probably has other issues it's dealing with.)

A tree knows that every season of its life is equally beautiful. That's why it stands just as proudly in the fall as in the spring. It's content no matter what the season. It doesn't try to change its fall colors into summer colors or wear its spring colors after autumn has set in. It takes each season as it comes and appreciates its beauty for what it is.

We could learn a lot from a tree.

There are only two ways to live your life. One is as though nothing is a miracle. The other is as though everything is a miracle.
—Albert Einstein

40

The Search

I tried killing a spider today. I squashed it three times with my shoe but it bounced right back. That's when I realized it was a dust ball.

I think my age is starting to affect my eyesight.

Mistaking a dust ball for a spider may be a more common occurrence than one might think. I'm sure many middle-agers have made the same incorrect assessment. Mistaking a dust ball for a cat, however, would not only mean I need a new pair of glasses but also the entire crew of Molly Maids.

A good friend of mine warned me that sometime after forty my eyesight would change. He said I would be reading the newspaper, a magazine, or a book and all of a sudden the letters would start running together. "Congress passes tax cut" would become "Fuphmfi hkswop ruilizhs." Either version would still be hard to believe.

My friend was right, though. Once I hit forty, my vision did change, and it seemingly happened overnight. I went to bed with 20/20 vision, and by breakfast I couldn't read the morning paper unless someone was holding it ten feet away.

OK, it's not quite that bad, but I am up to a 2 percent magnification in drugstore glasses. My optometrist is the one who recommended I buy my glasses at the drugstore. He told me if 2 percent was all the magnification I needed, why not spend $10 instead of $100? I like my optometrist. Of course, he's one of the last medical professionals still driving a Pacer.

My biggest problem with glasses is remembering to keep them with me. I've left them at work, at church, at restaurants, at department stores, at gas stations. The most common place I leave them, though, is on top of my head. I can never find them there. It's the last place I look.

What I want to know is why we don't lose other things on top of our head. When's the last time you saw someone walking around with a curling iron on her head, looking for her curling iron? Or her brush. Or a football helmet. That's because you usually don't forget when those things are up there. The curling iron is a bit unwieldy, a brush might be a possibility, but a football helmet? Well, you'd just know. So why is it so easy to lose our glasses up there? I guess it's just one of those unexplained phenomena of life.

I should probably buy one of those little dishes they make

especially for glasses. You know, the ones that say something clever like "Here they are, stupid." But I'm afraid a dish to hold my glasses would be just as easy to misplace.

Maybe they should start equipping eyeglasses with tracking devices. Then as soon as we realize our glasses are missing, we could call a central number, report the disappearance, and within seconds our glasses would start beeping.

Of course, if they are on top of your head, all the beeping could really give you a migraine.

I would never have amounted to anything were
it not for adversity.
—J. C. (James Cash) Penney

41

Scars

Most of us don't make it through life without a few scars. Over the years we've scraped a knee or two, maybe even broken a few bones. Life, though full of wonder and excitement, also comes with its share of pain.

When our youngest son was just two years old, he had to undergo two separate heart surgeries. The first was to repair what is called a patent ductus; the second was open-heart surgery to repair a ventricular septal defect.

After the first surgery was performed successfully, the doctor informed me in the Intensive Care Unit that the second surgery needed to be done within a few weeks. I wasn't prepared for that news. We had just made it through one grueling ordeal and now we were going to turn around and do it all over again. I had been hoping for more of a breather. I couldn't understand why the second surgery couldn't wait for at least a year or so.

One of the reasons the medical team felt they couldn't wait any longer than a few weeks was the fact that adhesions would start to form after the first surgery and these make a second incision more difficult. So we braced up for the second go-around in a few short weeks. Thankfully it was the right decision and all went well.

Did you know that the emotional wounds we suffer in life can also form adhesions around them? These make it difficult for help to get through—not impossible, however. God's love can cut through even the toughest scars.

If you've been scarred by an abusive or controlling parent, sibling, spouse, or even a friend, or if you've suffered some other traumatic incident in your life, chances are you've developed some adhesions to protect that wounded area. These may prevent further injury, but they also keep you from making repairs on the inside. In this second half of your life, maybe it's time to allow God to do what he does best—cut through those adhesions and mend your heart and spirit. The longer you wait, the tougher the scars become.

An unexamined life is not worth living.
—Socrates

42

Hold Your Tongue

I remember the very first time someone called me "ma'am." I was only in my twenties, but it felt like I had just been wished a happy birthday by Willard Scott.

Until that night, I had always been referred to as "girl," "hon," "sweetie," maybe even an occasional "Hey, you!" But now I was being called ma'am. *Ma'am*. There's no way to put a youthful spin on ma'am.

"Lady" is about as bad. The first time I heard "lady" in reference to me was jarring, too.

"Hey, lady, do you know that's wet cement you just parked in?"

I looked around. *Surely he can't be talking to me*, I thought. I was no lady. I was a *girl*. But since he was looking straight at me, and since my car did indeed seem to be just spinning its wheels, obviously stuck in something, I figured the title must have been intended for me.

Men don't have this problem. Addressing a teenage boy as "sir" is usually considered a compliment. You can be a sir at six as easily as at sixty.

We women, however, aren't in that much of a hurry to get to the "ma'am stage," so don't rush us.

I suppose it all evens out when we get into our senior years. People go back to calling us "sweetie," "hon," and "Hey, you!" again.

We might even get a few "Hey, babes" tossed in our direction. I wouldn't mind that. It would remind me that I've still got it. Now, if only I could remember what "it" is and where I put it!

Youth is happy because it has the ability to see beauty. Anyone who keeps the ability to see beauty never grows old.
—Franz Kafka

43

Running Hot and Cold

Circulation problems can sometimes develop as we grow older. Our blood still flows, it just takes it a little longer to make its rounds.

Lately I've started having some mild circulatory problems. I've got body parts falling asleep at all hours of the day and night, which I don't really think is fair. Why should I be getting only seven or eight hours of sleep a night while my right leg is getting twelve?

Circulation problems can also cause our body's thermostat to malfunction. We'll often find ourselves feeling colder than anyone else. You start to realize this when you look around and notice you're the only one on the beach wearing a parka.

I'll admit my body temperature runs substantially colder than anyone else in our house. My teeth will be chattering and I'll have lost all feeling in my feet while everyone else is opening windows and putting ice packs on their heads to cool off.

I get cold everywhere—the house, the car, lava pits. Frankly, I think someone should come out with a personal mini-heater. You know, like those mini-fans you can hold in your hand. Personal mini-heaters could be used on airplanes, in cars, at the workplace, and most importantly, in grocery stores—they could distribute them to customers just before they embark down the frozen-food aisle.

I could really use a mini-heater at home. My husband, lord of the thermostat, likes to keep our house set at sixty-eight degrees. When he's not looking, I usually turn it up just a bit, somewhere between "Three Mile Island" and "Volcano."

Thus begins our "Dance of the Thermostat." My husband takes the lead. First, he turns, slides four steps to the left, stretches his arm up John Travolta-style, and deftly turns the thermostat down. I pivot on one foot, take three steps to the right, do a backbend, and turn it back up. He takes my hand, twirls me in two complete revolutions, leads me eight steps away, and moonwalks back to the thermostat to turn it down again.

The dance is really quite interesting to watch. Once in a while one of the kids will try to cut in and set the thermostat where they want it, but it's not long before it's just my husband and me again, freezing and sweating and dancing until dawn. How romantic!

It's too bad Arthur Murray never offered courses in the Dance of the Thermostat. He could have made a fortune.

Lord Tyrawley and I have been dead these two years, but we don't choose to have it known.
—Lord Chesterfield

44

That's Entertainment?

My taste in music has changed over the years. Not that I've become a die-hard polka fan or have the world's largest collection of Lawrence Welk music videos or anything like that, but I don't listen to the same music I used to listen to, either.

These days I prefer "easy listening"—that's all those songs you hear while riding elevators or getting your teeth drilled. I'm not all that fond of most of today's rock music. Often the lyrics are too explicit, and I don't like all that bass. If I want to get my heart pounding, there are other ways to do it, like finishing that sit-up I started last week.

I don't think I'd ever be able to get into the punk rock scene, either. Mosh pits don't entice me in the least. All that pushing and shoving and bumping into each other. I get enough of that at after-Christmas sales.

I do like country music, though. I like songs that tell a story, even if it is about some poor guy's wife getting trampled to death by an elephant at the circus and how the ringmaster sends him the bill for the elephant's therapy sessions after such trauma. Life's tough. Singing about it is how we cope.

My taste in movies has changed, too. I don't enjoy sophomoric humor or watching the antics of some seventeen-year-old heartthrob who thinks a liver spot is a stain you get on your shirt during dinner. I prefer complicated plots, good dialogue, and a forty-year-old heartthrob.

And there's been a change in what I read. I've traded in *Teen Beat* and *Seventeen* for *Newsweek* and *Time*, and I'll take an occasional peek at *Modern Maturity* (in a plain brown wrapper, of course).

Yet even though my taste in entertainment has changed over the years, I'm still the same person. The basic elements of one's personality don't change. If we were easygoing and reserved in our youth, we'll probably be easygoing and reserved in our later years. By the same token, if we were the adventurous daredevil type in our twenties, we'll still be the adventurous daredevil type when we reach our seventies. In other words, we'll be the one hang gliding off the patio at "the home."

Experience is the name that everyone gives to
their mistakes.
—Oscar Wilde

45

Made to Last

I recently attended the thirty-third California International Antiquarian Book Fair, which was held at a hotel near Los Angeles International Airport. My friend Cynthia Christenssen had invited me to go along with her. I had never been to an antiquarian book fair before, and it was fascinating to see the vast collection of rare and antique books.

One display especially caught my eye. It was a handful of pages from an old writing book that had been used by Mark Twain. There in his very own handwriting was part of one of Twain's manuscripts, complete with corrections. It was fascinating—and, of course, priced well into the thousands of dollars.

Many of the books at the show were in the same price neighborhood. There was one collection by Chaucer that was selling for, I believe, $250,000. My Visa card doesn't go that high. I couldn't have bought the bookmark that went along with it.

It was interesting, though, to watch people walk from booth to booth, surveying the rare and old books with respect and excitement. One book was 350 years old. Another was 200. There were books we remembered from our childhood (not the 200 one, of course). Rare book dealers had come from as far away as England, Germany, Spain, and countless other countries to display their collections and offer them for sale. If anyone had brought a book in that was less than ten years old, I don't think it would have gotten past the front gate.

So what makes these old and used books so valuable? Much of the reason has to do with the simple fact that they've survived. It's not easy to preserve a book for forty or fifty years, much less hundreds. They've seen too many yard sales, swap meets, and, of course, two-year-olds. Many books can't take it and eventually succumb to the wear and tear.

People are like books. Our pages may tear or turn yellow and our binding become loose. Some of our ideas might even sound dated or passé. But if we can somehow hold ourselves together, survive the elements to which life exposes us, and keep most of our pages intact, we'll have become a rare and special book indeed.

Keep away from people who try to belittle your
ambitions. Small people always do that, but the
really great make you feel that you, too,
can become great.
—Mark Twain

46

What'd You Say?

My husband suffered some hearing damage in his years of service with the Los Angeles Police Department. Today officers are required to wear ear protectors while qualifying with their service revolver. That wasn't the case when my husband joined the department, so the monthly visits to the firing range took their toll, and now he's paying for it.

High-pitched sounds are what give him the most trouble, especially background noises at restaurants and women's voices. Even with hearing damage, though, he refuses to get a hearing aid. I don't understand this thinking, but he's not alone. A lot of people think a hearing aid will make them look older than they want to look. Frankly, I don't get it. Does answering the question "Did the mail come?" with "No, I didn't see the cow" really make a person look younger?

Though my husband's hearing was damaged years ago, hearing loss is also a side effect of aging. And we don't only start losing our hearing, but our ears seem to get bigger, too. They continue to grow as we age, some of them even turning outward. Maybe that's to give us more access for trimming ear hairs?

I've found, though, that what most middle-aged and older people suffer most from is selective hearing. They hear what they want to hear. My husband can hear me whisper a Home Shopping Network order into the telephone from two rooms away, but he can't hear me calling him to dinner.

He can hear the rear fender of my car barely tap the planter as I'm backing out of the driveway—while he's taking a shower in the house—but he can't hear the telephone ringing when he's two feet away from it.

One of these days someone's going to come out with a chip for hearing aids that would work like the V-chip in a TV. It could be programmed to edit out all the things you don't want to hear: "Honey Do" lists, mother-in-law visiting plans, and long distance service sales pitches, to name a few. The advantages would be endless.

Until then, if we want to get out of uncomfortable situations, I guess we'll just have to keep on faking it.

He's so old that when he orders a three-minute
egg, they ask him for the money up front.
—Milton Berle

47

Who Unplugged the Fountain of Youth?

People have searched for it for years, and in case you're one of those still looking for it, I'm sorry to inform you that there is no fountain of youth. There is no pool of magical water where you can go for a dip and regain your youthful vitality. There are no water springs that will grant sharper memory or tighter skin. And if there were such a place, we wouldn't be able to get near it anyway. Can you imagine the parking problems?

No matter how badly we may want our youth to return, it's not coming back. Oh, we can snip a little here or tape a little back there, successfully taking a decade or so off our appearance, but we're not fooling Mother Nature. Once spent, youth can't be recaptured. We only get one dip in it, one go-around. Fountains of youth and time machines make interesting books and movies, but they are purely fictional.

I'm not so sure a fountain of youth would be a good idea anyway. Would we really want a world in which no one grew old? What kind of an existence would it be where we were all eternally adolescent? After a while we'd get tired of the childish games and rock music. We'd long for more variety, more substance, and some of the wisdom that only comes with age.

I once attended a church that had a young pastor and only a handful of older members. There was plenty of youthful energy there, but something important was missing. I like to call it the "been-there-survived-that mentality." I don't know about you, but I appreciate it when I'm going through a difficult time and an older adult shares with me that she, too, went through a similar difficulty and made it to the other side. It gives me hope.

So don't waste your time searching for the fountain of youth. Youthfulness isn't what you're seeking anyway, it's usefulness, and that isn't found in a fountain. It's only found within yourself.

The minute you settle for less than you deserve, you get even less than you settled for.
—Maureen David

48

Evading the Obvious

I once attended a memorial service in which the person delivering the eulogy did everything she could to avoid saying the word "dead." She used words like "departed, passed on, no longer with us, away, on the other side, gone to a better place, at peace, at rest, sleeping, walking with the angels"—well, you get the idea.

Most of us are uncomfortable talking about death. It's not something we put on our list of New Year's resolutions of things we want to do. We realize it's a natural part of the life cycle, but we don't like to dwell on it.

As we get older, though, the concept of death becomes harder and harder to ignore. We've attended far more funerals than we would have liked, and the fact that life has no guarantees is a truth that always seems to be slapping us in the face.

We may have even experienced a few brushes with death. My first close call came when I was only three months old. It was Christmas Eve, and my family had just left my uncle's house, heading for our home just a few miles away. While stopped at an intersection, we were struck head on by a drunk driver and knocked off the road and down an embankment.

Our car was totaled, and our injuries ranged from my father's critical condition to broken bones and bruises for most of the rest of us. One of those broken bones happened to be my arm. I easily could have been killed, though. But obviously God had a different plan for my life.

Then on a youth retreat as a teenager, I nearly drowned while playing underwater tag with our youth pastor. I didn't know how to swim, so every time he'd dive under the water to grab me, I'd take refuge by standing on his back. This seemed like a good idea to me at the time, but he was of a different opinion. Something about needing to breathe. Each time I stood on his back, he'd carry me for as long as he could, then finally knock me off so he could—breathe.

Once when he knocked me off, though, we were in nine feet of water, and down I went. I could hear voices laughing and talking in the background, but no one seemed to notice I was drowning. All I could do was pray and try not to open my mouth while doing so. The only parts of my body I could raise out of the water were my hands. I tried waving them, but still no one noticed my plight.

On my fourth attempt to rise to the surface, no part of my body cleared the water. That was when I began to accept the fact that it was over. I wasn't happy about it, mind you. Drowning was not on the list of retreat activities. But there wasn't a thing I could do to help myself.

Finally, someone yelled, "Hey, look, she's drowning!" From the moment I heard those words, I knew everything was going to be OK. I was still sinking like a rock in nine feet of water, but I now had hope.

Our youth pastor swam over to me and pulled me up and to the side of the pool, thus saving my life. I easily could have drowned that day. But God had a different plan for my life.

In the years that have followed, I've had other brushes with death. I'm sure you could relate some of your own. Arriving at an intersection four seconds earlier, you might have been hit by that car running the red light. Taking a closer look at the prescription spared you from swallowing someone else's medication.

Each of us may have missed death hundreds of times without even being aware of it.

Only God knows precisely how much time he's assigned us. There's no drop-in company in heaven. We're not going to get there a day sooner than he's expecting us. So whether we've been given forty-five years or ninety, it's up to us not to waste a single second of it.

Many of life's failures are people who did not
realize how close they were to success
when they gave up.
—Thomas A. Edison

49

And Another Thing . . .

A character's dying words are usually pretty moving—in the movies. Their lines have been brilliantly scripted by a screenwriter. They are concise yet poignant. There's no redundancy or bad grammar. You won't hear any clichés uttered on a deathbed on the big screen. The writer will give his character something memorable to say, something that will put the audience in awe of his wisdom at such a time.

It doesn't always happen that way in real life, though. Most of us don't wax eloquent when we're taking that final breath. On his deathbed, H. G. Wells uttered these memorable last words: "Go away. I'm all right." Pancho Villa was even less prepared for his final sentiment. He said, "Don't let it end like this. Tell them I said something." Convicted murderer James Rodgers had a little more time to think about what he would say before his death. When asked for his final request before facing the firing squad, he said, "Why, yes—a bulletproof vest."

Dying people have left us with brilliant insights as to the meaning of life. They've used their final words to reconcile broken relationships not only with people but also with their God. They've even used their last breath to utter revisions to their will, especially if their beloved beneficiary is standing at their bedside with a date.

When it comes time for me to utter my last words, I'm afraid I won't be able to do it. As a writer, I know I'm going to keep wanting to do a rewrite. I can hear myself now: "Take time to stop and smell the roses." Too cliché. "I regret that I have but one life to give for my cooking." No good either. That would force an investigation into my refrigerator and perhaps even an autopsy. "Life—live it, love it, give back to it." Ummm . . . now that has some promise. But with my luck, when that time comes there won't be a single pen in the house.

I am a part of all that I have met.
—Lord Alfred Tennyson

50

Priorities

A lot of what we allow to consume our time and energy isn't really important, at least not in the big picture. So just in case we ever question whether or not something is worth all the attention we're giving it, the following chart is provided:

WORTH OUR TIME	NOT WORTH OUR TIME
A good book	A TV show with no redeeming qualities
Thankfulness	Selfishness
Appreciating others	Petty jealousies
Friends who stand by you	Friends who desert you
Helping others	Getting even with others
Encouraging people	Discouraging people
Spending time with family	Working unnecessary overtime

Taking a long walk	Waiting in long lines
Having a pet	Fretting over a neighbor's pet
Love	Hate
Striving for excellence	Striving to bury your competition
Peace of mind	Worry over things you can't control

What Youth deemed crystal,
Age finds out was dew.
—Robert Browning

51

The Ride

I remember as a child going to carnivals and amusement parks with my family. After waiting in long lines, some for nearly an hour, I'd climb onto the ride with so much excitement I could barely contain myself.

About halfway through the ride, though, my focus would change. Instead of enjoying the remainder of the ride, I could hardly wait for it to be over so I could rush back to the end of the line and ride it again.

I rarely paid any attention to the second half. All I could think about was how much fun it was going to be the next time around. Or the third time. Or the fourth.

I'm sure I missed out on a lot of fun during the second half of those rides. Those who design amusement parks don't put all the thrills in the first half of a ride. They usually design them to be an exciting experience from start to finish. In fact, the second half is often the best part of the ride. The fun is there to be enjoyed. If we're not paying attention, there's no one to blame but ourselves.

Life can be like an amusement park ride. It can be a series of gently paced ups and downs like a merry-go-round, or it can be a roller coaster adventure from start to finish with lots of exhilarating highs and breathtaking lows. Wherever the ride takes us or how much we choose to enjoy it, one thing is for certain: There is no second go-around. We can't hop off this ride and run to the back of the line and do it again. We only get one ticket. When our ride in this world is over, that's it—for this portion of the adventure anyway.

If you're over forty, chances are you're at the halfway point of the ride. Barring accidents, many, if not most of us, will live to be seventy or eighty or beyond. That means we've got just as many years left to live as we've already lived. So we shouldn't rush through it. If we close our eyes during the second half of this ride, we might be missing out on what could very well be the very best part.

"The Lord bless you and keep you; the Lord
make his face shine upon you and be gracious to
you; the Lord turn his face toward you and
give you peace."
—Numbers 6:24–26 NIV

Thank you for selecting a book from
BETHANY HOUSE PUBLISHERS

Bethany House Publishers is a ministry of Bethany Fellowship International, an interdenominational, nonprofit organization committed to spreading the Good News of Jesus Christ around the world through evangelism, church planting, literature distribution, and care for those in need. Missionary training is offered through Bethany College of Missions.

Bethany Fellowship International is a member of the National Association of Evangelicals and subscribes to its statement of faith. If you would like further information, please contact:

Bethany Fellowship International
6820 Auto Club Road
Minneapolis, MN 55438 USA